Search for Peace

Search for Peace

THE POLITICS OF THE MIDDLE GROUND
IN THE ARAB EAST

HASSAN BIN TALAL
Crown Prince of Jordan

St. Martin's Press
New York

ISBN: 0–312–70821–1

Library of Congress Catalog Number: 84–51212

First Published in Great Britain by Macmillan London Limited

First U.S. Edition

10 9 8 7 6 5 4 3 2 1

His Majesty King Hussein of Jordan with his
brother Crown Prince Hassan

Contents

Acknowledgements

No book is written without the help and assistance of others and this one is no exception. I am deeply indebted for the contributions of Mr Nicolas Barker, Dr Ahmad Mango and Dr Abbas Kelidar who read and commented on the original manuscript. Special thanks are also due to Dr Bassam al-Saket and Brigadier Ali El-Edroos as well as to the Research Unit at my office. For the diligent typing of several copies of the manuscript, thanks must be expressed to Miss Mary Jordan, Mrs Jacky Sawalha and Mrs Sally Dale.

There must be, not a balance of power, but a community of power; not organised rivalries, but an organised peace.

Woodrow Wilson
Address to the United States Senate
22 January 1917

To the martyrs of the Arab Renaissance Movement.

Introduction

Who are the Palestinians, the Lebanese, the Jordanians, the Syrians or the Iraqis, whether Christians or Muslims? Are they the descendants of those who led the Pan-Arab Renaissance Movement of seventy years ago and the recipients of its principles and ideals? If so, why is it that they seem to have forsaken all semblance of solidarity, let alone unity, in the face of adversity? These are pertinent questions that all Arabs are asking as they confront the major crises of today, which threaten their very existence as a people, not to say the several nation states that they occupy. From the Mediterranean to the Gulf, wars have been waged against the Arab national identity. Iran in the east and Israel in the west seek to eradicate the ethnic identity of the Arab people, each answering an alien call that generations of Arabs have consistently rejected. Both Iran and Israel want to impose their hegemony on the Arab people through the fragmentation of the Arab community of states and the return of their societies to the long-dead condition of warring and feuding tribes.

There is a need for a serious examination of the obstacles that have thwarted our dream of unity and caused us to revert to the basic common bond of ethnic, sectarian or ideological affiliations. There must be a clear-sighted definition of the goals set out by the Hashemite political leadership for more than half a century. There is a great richness in diversity. Pluralism in society and politics is a noble aim. It should not be a cause for disunity but a basis for the evolution of a well-integrated and harmonious commonwealth. The question that faces us is this: do we still have the political will to overcome our differences and achieve a common identity

1

based on a *terra media* of interests in an increasingly polarized world? If we are to survive we will have to muster that will. We must possess the intellectual generosity to rekindle these ideals if politics are to be conducted, as politics must be, for the benefit of the people.

It pains me as it must pain every Arab to see the Arab world beset by so many problems, so much dissent and conflict. From the Gulf to the Atlantic the overall pattern appears to be one of inter-Arab disputes and conflicts. We would do well to recall the words of Count Bernadotte, a man who gave his life for the sake of peace in the Middle East, when he said, "The position of the Arabs . . . is confused and confusing". To him, it was "axiomatic", as it is to us, that no solution to the question of Palestine could satisfy both Jews and Arabs. The late King Abdullah, my grandfather, who also fell as a martyr to the cause of peace, came to the conclusion that a unanimous Arab position on this vital matter was difficult to achieve. Although some significant shifts have taken place, the essential element of this drama has changed but little. Impasse and deadlock still seem to be the salient features of the situation in the Middle East.

The Palestinians have developed a sense of their own particular nationalism; yet, in the main, they still look to the Arab world for succour and sustenance. They have failed to set up a state of their own and have been deprived of the right to self-determination. On the other side, the Jews have founded a state to the existence and security of which almost all nations, including the superpowers, subscribe. Israel, however, has not been placed in the context of the region to which it claims to belong. It is questionable, indeed, whether Israel wishes to be a part of the Middle East. After the death and destruction that have accompanied the invasion of Lebanon, Israel appears determined to become a dominating minority in an ever-growing mosaic of ethnic communities.

Armed force and its use have characterized Israel's reaction to the crisis in the Middle East. Israel has constantly rejected the notion of national self-determination for the Palestinians, on the premise that a people without a country cannot entertain such a right. Military campaigns have been conduc-

2

ted to destroy the Palestinian sense of Arab identity, without success. It is self-evident that brute force, and the acquisition of territory by its use, is conducive neither to peace nor to the peaceful resolution of the Middle East problem. It can only lead to the intensification of radical trends, particularly of the fundamentalist variety, in these societies. The appeal of the politico-religious movement in both Arab and Israeli societies is simple and can be extremely effective. The only outcome of the present Israeli stance is the erosion of the politics of the middle ground where moderation, tolerance and co-operation prevail.

The Arabs, in all their different political hues, cannot resolve their differences. More tragic still, Jew and Arab cannot desegregate themselves of their own volition. Hilaire Belloc, the renowned British writer, spoke of the Jewish race as a whole as having been "inspired by as strong a motive as can move men to action, but", he cautioned, "this strength alone would not maintain the Jews against the fierce hostility of the Moslem world which surrounds them". That hostile sense has been enhanced by Israel's attitude and action. It has become a moral force that will predominate in the future unless greater wisdom and foresight predominate in the conduct of public affairs. Belloc went on to say that, in the West, hostility towards the Jews is not appreciated because it is no longer heard of, but, "if we ignore it, we are ignoring something which may change our fate".

The solution of the Palestine question is central to the stability of the Middle East. Yet it is often asserted in the West, and more particularly in the United States, that a uniform policy towards the crisis in the region cannot be formulated because of the divergent interests of the many parties concerned. It is certainly true that Arab states, whose governance has been shattered by *coups d'état* and the frequent resort to violence in the settlement of domestic political disputes, maintain different positions on a powerful and emotive national cause. However, what is essentially required is a direct, positive redress to the Palestinian grievances. It goes without saying that the resolution of any dispute hinges upon the redress offered to the injured party. If the

Palestinians are content with the terms of a settlement, it would not matter if other Arabs were to object, no matter who they might be.

There is a prevalent tendency to segregate the oil-producing zones of the Arabian peninsula from the states to the north of it, whose wealth lies in manpower. It is not only in the interest of the Arabs, but of the whole world, that this should be resisted. The deliberate distancing of the more populous, more volatile states of the north – Iraq, Syria, Jordan and Lebanon – from the more phlegmatic Gulf states with their vulnerable resources has been virtually achieved. As the Gulf region becomes increasingly introverted, it is appropriate to point out their need for reinforcement. Our hopes and aspirations should not be separated from the considerable resources which are Arab in origin and environment, but are not administered in accordance with a joint Arab economic strategy for the benefit of all the inhabitants of the area.

Given the strategic interests expressed by the superpowers in the Middle East, and the current deterioration in East-West relations, the Middle East is liable to become a flashpoint for a global confrontation. It could easily ignite a conflagration of international violence. It has already intensified polarization and undermined regional independence and national sovereignty. The West has interests vital to its security and well-being in the region. Sixty per cent of West European and Japanese oil imports originate from the Gulf region alone. The sea lanes pass through the "choke point" of the Hormuz Straits. The economic and strategic importance of our region to the West is self-evident. Yet, we are puzzled, confused, disorientated and disillusioned at the lack of direction and decisiveness in the formulation of Western, especially American, policy. The region is crying out for a new initiative and a positive, more determined, approach to our problems, but all we receive is evasion, procrastination and prevarication.

I believe that patterns of history do recur. In 1918 Balfour, reflecting on the Sykes-Picot Agreement of 1916, foresaw the assignment of a role to the Americans in the post-war settlement and said, "If they choose to step in and cut the knot, that

is their affair, but we must not put the knife into their hand."
Today the knife is there, poised to cut: we need an American
president who can say, "Let us start with a clean slate." The
unscrupulous secret agreements and *Realpolitik* of half a century have only brought misery to the people of our region. My
generation has lived all its life under the shadow of war and
uncertainty. President Woodrow Wilson, the champion of
self-determination for peoples, once offered hope to the Arabs.
This call has been echoed by the Hashemites since the Peace
of Versailles. The four chapters of this book are a sincere plea
for a better understanding of the Arab search for peace. They
attempt to answer the questions that all Arabs ask: "Who am
I?" "To whom do I belong?" and "How shall I face the
future?" My purpose in this work is to break down the
stereotyped patterns that have vexed all previous discussion
and action, and to humanize the image and issues that
constitute the major concerns in the Arab East today. Politics
is also about people, and it is the hopes and needs of the people
of the region that I am to articulate.

1 The Arabs: an Historical Sketch

In the modern world the Arab stands out as a curiously disoriented creature among other races and nations. That traditional figure, the nomad tending his camels, the lifeline of desert transport, is not extinct: yet beside him is his modern equivalent, just as dependent on the jet, whether he be oil-rich sheikh or poor pilgrim. The paradox goes beyond modes of travel or the undreamt wealth that some Arabs command and the miserable poverty that others suffer. The Arab is an individualist with a yearning for unfettered liberty, resisting all forms of constraint or restraint; yet, more often than not, he is the prisoner of a tradition-bound society, the historic legacy of a way of life rooted in Islam and, beyond Islam, in time immemorial. The Arab of today is a citizen of many nation-states, all recently created; but he prefers to trace his genealogy back far enough to establish his position in the common bank of tribal affiliations that transcend the modern political frontiers now separating him from his fellow Arabs. He realizes his Arabism as much as he reveres Islam and observes the religious obligations that it imposes on him. This mixture of tradition and modernity has shown that, despite the remote harshness of desert life, the Arab has not been isolated or confined to his oasis. He is not a sterile creature devoid or unaware of civic culture, as he is sometimes portrayed. Hostile though his modern surroundings may be, no amount of denigration and belittlement will force the individual Arab to abandon his traditional way of life. He has always been, and will remain, in one of the main streams of the cultural tradition of mankind, varied and changing as it has been over the centuries.

Pre-history

Not much of the early history of the Arabs is known. Our present knowledge is derived from an assortment of sources. While the history of the three centuries before Islam is based almost wholly on Muslim tradition and some pre-Islamic Nabatean and Arabic inscriptions, far earlier records of a distinct Arab race can be found in Assyrian records and the chronicles of classical writers.

It is of considerable interest to historians that the term "Arab", indicating a particular human group or a specific ethnic community, can be traced to the most ancient historical sources. The tenth chapter of *Genesis* contains references to the Arabs, as do Assyrian and Babylonian inscriptions, which make frequent mention of *Aribi*, *Arabu* and *Uribi*. These records are accompanied by illustrations of the people. The presence of the camel, the symbol of nomadic life, in these illustrations provides a further indication of the identity of the people, the wandering tribes of northern Arabia. In Persian cuneiform documents, the term *Arabaya* is used in the same sense as the later Greek and Latin histories employed it to signify the geographical area of the Arabian peninsula and its inhabitants.

In Arabia, the topography of the land determined the nature of human settlement. There are the undulating plains and slopes of the Tihama region along the Red Sea, the mountain range of Hijaz separating the coastal plains from the Najd hinterland, and the inland plateau of Najd consisting mainly of enormous shifting sand dunes, known as al-Nufud, in the north and the vast impenetrable deserts of al-Rub al-Khali to the south. There are the areas of solid ground nearer Syria and Iraq, known as the Hamad. North of the peninsula lies the fertile crescent of Syria and Iraq, whose terrain has dictated a different pattern of culture and made the region the bridge that linked the Western world with the East. Religion and culture made this region the hub of the universe and the cradle of the civilization we know today.

The configuration of the land established certain well-defined routes along which human beings could move and trade could therefore follow. The first was along the Red Sea ports, linking southern Syria, Jordan and Palestine with the Yemen through Hijaz. The second route ran through Wadi al-Rum to southern Iraq and Jordan. These were the major lines of communication in ancient times between the southern Arabian civilization of the Yemen and those of ancient Syria and Iraq in the north, and the world outside Arabia, both to the east and to the west. Syria was further linked with central Arabia via Wadi Sirhan and the Jawaf oases.

Although the basic social unit remained essentially the tribe, and the movement of tribes followed the trade routes, there was a certain degree of difference between the Arabs of southern Arabia and those of the north. The southern Arabs were sedentary people engaged in agriculture, which gave Arabian spices their famous reputation in the annals of the peoples of the Mediterranean. The Arabs of the north, however, remained nomadic and largely dependent on the camel. Both were influenced by the commercial contacts that transformed purely tribal settlements into a sophisticated political community. Both the southern and northern Arab communities, based at the centre of these huge commercial networks, became states which held sway to a large degree over the neighbouring areas. Both served as the means by which alien social and cultural influences penetrated Arab life.

In the south was the kingdom of Sab'a, the Sheba whose Queen visited Solomon in the Bible, and the Himyarite civilization. In the north, the main influence on the Arab settlements came from the hellenized Aramaic culture of Syria. The most important of these northern Arabs were the Nabateans, whose domain extended from the Gulf of Aqaba to the Dead Sea and included much of the northern Hijaz. Their capital was the renowned Petra in southern Jordan, and their King was Haritha, known to Greek historians as Aretas. Petra was the base from which the Emperor Augustus launched his campaign in 25–24 BC for the conquest of Yemen and control of the lucrative trade route – the incense trail – to India. There were other border states. In AD 265, Uthaina (Odenathus) established an independent state at Palmyra which Queen Zenobia made famous. The government of all these societies was based on kingship with a regular succession by primogeniture. The kings were not regarded as divine, since their religion was the traditional polytheism common to all the Semitic cultures of the time. All these states on the periphery of the Arab peninsula were Nabatean; their culture and language were Aramaic; their Arab character is revealed only in their names.

By the sixth century AD Arab border kingdoms replaced those of the Nabateans, thus exposing traditional Arab society to a more direct and intensive cultural influence from the outside world. Like their predecessors the Romans, who had encouraged the rise of the Nabateans and Palmyran domains, the Byzantine Empire in the west and the Empire of the Sasanides in the east encouraged and induced the emergence of the two Arab states of Ghassan and Hira on the Arabian frontiers of Syria and Iraq respectively.

The Ghassanides established their kingdom in the vicinity of the Yarmouk river in southern Syria and northern Palestine. Recognition of their independent status was conceded by the Byzantine Emperors, who recognized rather than appointed their rulers. The principality of Hira on the border of the Sasanide Empire could not claim such a position. Its status was more dependent on the strength and weakness of its rulers relative to the Sasanide Emperors, independent when they were strong and vassals when they were weak. Hira enjoyed a period of great independence under its ruler Munthir III, a contemporary of the Ghassanide Harith who was made a phylarch and a patrician by Justinian.

Both Ghassan and Hira were Christian states, the former Monophysite and the latter Nestorian. Both had a tincture of Aramaic and Hellenistic culture, some of which to some degree permeated further to the interior of the peninsula. Ghassan, on the eve of the rise of Islam, was deprived of its financial subsidies from Byzantium: the old links with the West were broken and unrest was widespread. When the Arab Muslims of the south invaded Ghassanide territory, the welcoming gates were wide open. The Arab kingdom of Hira, although a vassal of the Persians, had always considered itself closer to the western kingdom and had drawn its culture mainly from the West, from the Hellenic tradition and Christian civilization of Syria. In consequence, the call of Arab Islam was heard in Hira and proved so pervasive that not only Iraq but Persia itself came under its sway.

Nomadism, we have seen, was the dominant feature of life amongst the Bedouin tribes of Arabia. The Arab's love of liberty and the freedom to roam in search of his livelihood was the product of his desert environment. He had a natural reluctance to accept any constraint on his movement. Yet, paradoxically, individuality could only flourish within a close social group. Each member of the community, whether it was a clan or tribe or, indeed, as we shall see, the community of Islam, had rights and obligations by virtue of his association with other individuals. While Islam introduced new bases for the Arabian community, the group maintained its unity, bound externally by the need for defence against hostile neighbours and the dangers of harsh desert life, and internally by the blood-tie of descent through the male line.

Complete tribal nomadism gave way to the sedentary pattern of social life in the oasis. These small communities formed rudimentary political organizations in which the leading family would prevail and establish its rule over the local inhabitants. A ruler could obtain further control over the neighbouring areas, so that a large tribal confederation might be formed under the hegemony of one ruler and his family. The kingdom of Kinda, which flourished in the fifth and early sixth centuries AD in northern Arabia between and to the south of Ghassan and Hira, was perhaps the best example of such a development. Kinda, whose rulers described themselves as "Kings of all the Arabs", had to contend with the power and influence of both Byzantine and Sasanide Empires. Nevertheless, the kingdom succeeded, despite opposition, in uniting the Arab tribes: Arabic as spoken in Kinda became a common language above and beyond the different tribal dialects. A standardized poetic language and technique became one of its finest achievements.

The oasis apart, isolated towns were established by settled

nomads and these became important commercial and religious centres. Amongst the most important towns was Mecca in the Hijaz, which has maintained its paramount significance to the present day. In pre-Islamic Mecca the conduct of public affairs followed tribal modes of behaviour. Each tribe or clan had an elected leader known as a Shaykh or a Sayyid. The head was rarely more than first among equals. He followed, more often than led, tribal opinion. Rights and obligations attached to individual families within the tribe but to none outside. The function of the Shaykh was to arbitrate, rather than to command, within the framework of established tribal convention and precedent. He possessed few coercive powers, so that the concepts of authority and kingship, a system of law with public penalties, were not known in Arab nomad society.

The Shaykh was elected by the elders of the tribe, usually from among the members of a single family – a Shaykhly house known as Ahl al-Bayt. He was advised by a council of elders called the Majlis, consisting of the heads of families and representative clans within the tribe. The Majlis was the mouthpiece of public opinion. In Mecca a union or a federation of several Majlises (*Mijālis*) was formed. It was given tangible expression by the central shrine in Mecca, where each family had its sacred stone grouped round the Ka'ba, the black stone, the common symbol of all. The Ka'ba became the revered symbol of unity in Mecca. The conditional and consensual character of Shaykhly authority was gradually defined by the confederation of ruling families and restricted to the most numerous Quraish, the tribe of which the clan of the Prophet Muhammad, the Bani Hashim, my ancestors, was the most eminent.

The coming of Islam

The mission of Muhammad introduced the most fundamental transformation of Arab society. Islam is not just a religion for the individual Muslim. It is not simply an ideological doctrine or scripture. It is all those things and more. Islam has become the complex religious–cultural bond of a civilization which had absorbed many facets of the social, administrative and economic life of Byzantine Syria, of the philosophy of Persia and India, with a tincture of the Greek cultural tradition. All these diverse elements moulded together to form the Muslim civilization. Despite these complex and substantial adaptive processes, the Islamic tenets have remained essentially simple and clear enough to guide the millions of Muslims in their daily life.

What is surprising about the initial impact of Islam on Arab society is how little outward change was to be seen. The tribal system continued to prevail in towns and the less settled regions of Arabia. Indeed Muhammad faced a great deal of opposition from his fellow Meccans at the start of his mission. He was forced to withdraw to Medina, the second most important centre for Arabia and subsequently for all Muslims. It was at Medina that the Prophet was able to put his teachings into practice. What he did there was to be of lasting significance not only for the Arabs, but for mankind.

His primary aim was the creation of a new social entity. In it, the Islamic bond took precedence over all other loyalties. Social distinction was no longer to rest on an exclusively tribal or familial basis, but between those who believed in the prophecy of Muhammad and followed the instructions contained in the Revelation and those who did not. This notion crystallized later into the differentiation between Muslims and infidels. The "people of the Book", Jews and Christians of all denominations, were specifically excluded from the latter category. This tolerance was specially enjoined in the Koran itself, in the twenty-ninth Sura, *Al-Ankabut*, verse 46. Muslims, regardless of their tribal affiliations, were made equal and collectively responsible for the defence of their fellow Muslims – the Muslim community. Muhammad, the Prophet, was the final arbiter in any dispute among members of his community. In short, the first step towards establishing the Muslim state was the creation of a tribe-like social entity to be known as the Muslim Umma, with Muhammad as its chief. It was obvious that Islam did not require the abolition, all at once, of the old tribal structure. The initial stage was to modify and expand the existing tribal order so that it would meet the requirements of the new and larger community of Islam.

The most radical change that Islam introduced to the Arabs was that henceforward the ultimate authority for the well-being of the community rested not with their tribal chiefs or in their stone idols, nor on the collective will of the people, but with Muhammad and beyond him with Allah, the Omnipotent. This notion of where power lies constituted a profound change in Arab social life. It introduced for the first time a concept already familiar from contacts with neighbouring societies – namely, that of an overlord. The individuals who composed the Muslim community were made to relinquish a good part of their ancient freedom, to forego their free choice of a leader and to submit to divine authority. The tribal Arabs had, in effect, and for as long as the Prophet himself was alive, become a theocracy – a community of God. In this perfect and immutable order there is no distinction between spiritual and temporal realms. Both form a unity under *al-Sharia*, the all-embracing laws of Islam. As the Prophet was the source of the whole regulation of society, it followed that during his lifetime Muslims had no need to be concerned with the relation of different institutions in society or with where relative power lay. The nature of the indivisibility of Islam into religious and secular activities made it theoretically impossible for anyone to legislate once the Revelation was completed – that is, upon the death of Muhammad. Moreover, the Prophet derived his political authority not from tribal acknowledgement of his position but from his divine office, which could not be inherited or emulated.

The quandary in which Muslims found themselves after the death of the Prophet was soon resolved by devising an alternative arrangement for the government of the Muslim community, symbolized in the institution of the Caliphate. The word *Khalifa*, it must be emphasized, means "successor", the inheritor of the Prophet's *temporal* (not divine) power. It implies what it says – the importance of the continuity of tradition set out by the Prophet to posterity, which would lack the direction of the divine inspiration which was his alone. The Caliphate thus made provision for the two needs of Islam

14

after his death: the need for future legislation, and the need for succession. The legislative process had to follow an elaborate procedure, whereby all decisions had to be made in accordance with a formula based on three principles: *Qiyăs, Ijmà, Muslaha* – analogy, consensus and public interest. First, all resolutions must be decided by comparison with the pronouncement of the Prophet and his conduct in similar situations; second, they must be agreed upon by the leading men of the community as compatible with the basic tenets of religion; finally, they must be shown to serve the public interest.

The problem of succession was solved by the gradual evolution of two methods: the first was designation by one leading Muslim of another; the second was nomination by the incumbent of a successor. Both required public acknowledgement afterwards. There were other conditions and qualifications which a candidate had to possess. Among the most important has been descent from Quraish and the family of the Prophet through his daughter, which today my own Hashemite family represents. However, the various vicissitudes of the Muslim community in its long evolution involved the emergence of military chieftains in the farther parts of the Muslim empires. This in turn led to the usurpation of power by people who were not strictly speaking qualified to rule and lead the community. These Sultans (and military governors) established their rule in various places all over the Muslim world. The Ottoman Sultanate of Turkey proved eventually the longest lasting and most powerful. The conquest, in the sixteenth century, of the Hijaz led to the general assumption that the Ottoman Sultan was equivalent to the Caliph, although the Sultans did not assume the title until later, and did not actively manipulate the title for political purposes until the nineteenth century. Tension then began to grow because of the impossibility of reconciling the ideal Muslim view of state and society (see Chapter 2) with the systems of government which constituted actual temporal power.

The Muslim community from about the late ninth until the early nineteenth century had thus had to accommodate the reality of power and authority derived from the use of force.

This feature continued to dominate Muslim rule until the nineteenth century, when the Napoleonic invasion, and the traumatic fact of the occupation of traditionally Muslim land by non-Muslim forces, brought the whole issue of rule by temporal power into question. The Arabs came to the conclusion that the political leadership of Islam must be restored to its legitimate holders if the religion and its traditions were to survive in their original purity and simplicity. This kind of Arab religious assertion became entangled with European expansion and encroachment of Muslim lands. It also became associated with the idea of a new nationalism as it began to gather adherents among the Muslims of many nationalities. National identity became the symbol, while religious affiliation remained the instrument, of their resistance and struggle against foreign dominations.

The new nationalism and the impact of Europe

The dawn of the twentieth century marked the beginning of a new era for the Arab East in more senses than one. The previous century had seen changes in it more rapid than in any previous era, changes more substantial and disturbing than any it had had to accommodate before. Practically every facet of life was influenced in one way or another by the pervasive European influence, violent or peaceful, in the region. Although the countries of the Arab East had been the object of European cultural, commercial and political penetration for a long time, the strength of the new onslaught forced an equally violent reaction.

Throughout the nineteenth century, when European powers dominated almost the entire world, all the countries of the Arab East were, at least formally, part of the Ottoman Empire. But at the turn of the twentieth century the European states had made huge inroads. Britain controlled the virtually independent Khedive of Egypt, Russia was becoming a major power in the Muslim north and pushing feelers out into the enfeebled Persian empire, while the British government of India was dominant in the Gulf. In 1912 Italy invaded Libya, while France had been in an unchallengeable position for decades in the other North African countries, as well as powerful in nominally Ottoman Syria.

The political stirring experienced by the Arabs was not confined to them but was part of a movement that pervaded the whole of the Muslim world. The phenomenon was partly due to the instinctive reaction of a proud people against foreign rule and interference. Various European cultural influences left an indelible mark on Arab society and determined the nature of its political structures from that day to this, as many of these countries began to adopt a Western style of government. While Arabs, Muslims and non-Muslims wrestled with the legacy of their past in an attempt to rejuvenate their governing institutions and revitalize their inherited principles, there was a change in the international climate.

It was an ominous change, boding ill for a people on the threshold of an intellectual and spiritual renaissance, whose precepts were beginning to find expression in more concrete terms. It was about this time that the interests of almost all the European powers began to clash. The traditional rivals, Britain, France, Russia and Germany, were all waiting hungrily around the dying Ottoman Empire. This pressure caused considerable dislocation to the social order of a highly conservative, not to say tradition-bound society, since their methods of domination took different forms. Apart from the extra-territorial rights known as "capitulations", the European powers acquired economic concessions in the Arab provinces of the Ottoman Empire. Christian missionaries were active in the fields of education and public health. While the works of many European orientalists and travellers (some sympathetic and others hostile) prompted the need for a better understanding of Arab society and its basic characteristics, they also highlighted its weaknesses for the Arabs. All this caused a transformation in the outlook of the Arabs. Change and reform became inevitable.

By 1900 the European political scene had undergone a radical shift which was reflected in the politics of the Ottoman Empire. Britain, France and Russia, who had hitherto disputed the possession of influence and dominance in the Arab East, began to become aware of a new change in the relation of forces. The rise of German power and increasing German interest in the affairs of the dying Empire challenged the established pattern of relationship. In 1899 Germany obtained a preliminary concession from the Ottoman Sultan for the construction of the famous Baghdad–Berlin railway, which played an important role in the conduct of the First World War in the Arab East. The railway connected Baghdad and the Gulf with the German capital via Istanbul. The Germans also acquired the rights to develop other industries, particularly the oil fields of northern Iraq. Indeed, we can now see, with all the clarity of hindsight, that oil was an important consideration which forced the pace of European aggrandizement in the Middle East. Oil concessions were to determine the nature and extent of the various European zones of influence which divided the Arab East in the peace negotiations and the eventual settlement that followed the First World War.

Germany's aid brought with it political influence, as British and French aid had done before. The Germans proceeded to exploit their position in the Ottoman state. On his side, the Sultan hoped to make use of European rivalry and gladly accepted increased German activity within the boundaries of his far-flung Empire. Although it was a familiar pattern in the conduct of public affairs in the region, it served to agitate greater resentment among his subjects against both the Sultan and the foreign powers he was trying to play off against each other. Among the powers themselves, Britain was first disposed to look upon German encroachment as a counter-weight to Russian and French penetration, but the German threat was too real and serious to be ignored.

The scene changed quickly with the conclusion of the *Entente Cordiale* between Britain and France in 1904, whereby certain countries within the Ottoman state were acknowledged as respective zones of influence by the key powers. The Anglo-French agreement was followed by a similar convention between Britain and Russia in 1907, dividing Persia into a Russian-dominated area in the north, a British-controlled area in the south and with the Shah left in charge of a buffer zone in between. The purpose was to shut Germany out of the region as war began to threaten Europe. We can now see clearly that the dynamics of conflict in Europe and the politics of confrontation on what is now a global scale have been reflected time and again by similar reactions to the same problem. Nobody can miss the parallels between the "northern tier" concept of the present Western defence systems to contain and check the expansion of Soviet influence and the attempts of other European "owners" to limit German expansion before the First World War. Again, the attempts by the USSR to break out of the Western encirclement have been a major factor in the politics of polarization between the Great Powers since the end of the Second World War.

The impact of European power and encroachment on Muslim lands served to indicate the extent of the decline and weakness under which the Ottoman government had to labour in the conduct of international relations. Educated Ottomans, Turks, Arabs and others, Muslims and non-Muslims, began to look for ways to check and contain the domination by Western Europe in their homelands. Their attempts can be seen in the formulation of various ideologies. In most cases these formulations were borrowed from contemporary European political thought, with the object, ironically enough, of combating Europe. "Pan-Ottomanism", devised to prevent the increasing estrangement among the different ethnic communities of the Empire, soon gave way to "Pan-Islam". The new self-awareness generated by the Pan-Islamic movement among these communities now transformed into nationalism familiar as "Pan-Turan", or Turkism, and "Pan-Arab", or Arabism; with this came progressive acceptance of the nation-state. Thus the movement served as a catalyst for the break-up of the last multinational and multilingual Muslim domain in the history of Islam.

My sense of history is directly related to the role played by the Arabs in the long history of Muslim civilization and to the evolution of its governing institution, namely the Caliphate. Our long tradition of continuity has a direct bearing on the legitimate position of the Hashemite family both in Arab and Muslim societies over the centuries. Thus I feel no dichotomy between my attachment to Islam and the promotion of Arab national identity. It was in this spirit that my great-grand-father, Sharif Hussein of Mecca, felt bound in honour to assume the title of Caliph only when it was formally abandoned by the Turks in 1924. He did it for the external glory of Islam as much as for the Arabs, for he was well aware that his rule did not extend beyond the Arabian peninsula and the fertile crescent. These areas have always been considered the hub of the Arab world and the spiritual foundations of Islam. The same consideration prompted my grandfather, the late King Abdullah, to designate the administration he established in Jordan as *Imarat al-Sharq al-Arabi* – the Amirate of the Arab East – when he set out from Hijaz in 1920 to restore Hashemite rule over Syria. It was this Amirate that became the foundation of the Hashemite kingdom of Jordan when the British Mandate came to an end in 1946.

Nevertheless, the concept of nationalism among the Arabs has continued to be rather vague and sometimes even con-fused. The reason for this confusion is the repeated attempts of most ideologues of Arab nationalism to view the history of the Arabs not in the mould of the present but of the future. They have consistently argued that the Arab nation would not rise until the entire Muslim past is seen to conform to their own image of the present and the future. They have tried to force the past into the mould that is required to justify this vision, and have thus been inclined to deal with the Arab East not as it is but as it ought to be. The frustrations felt by succeeding generations of Arabs have been, as it were, built into the system of thought and, in consequence, attempts to reconstruct the basis of an Arab nation have failed for lack of proper foundations.

In their eagerness to recast the past in the image of the future, the ideologues of nationalism looked on every Arab assertion of their dominance in the long history of Islam as evidence of that nationalism. What this means, in effect, is the transformation of Islam from the universalist, egalitarian religion that the Prophet Muhammad intended for the whole of mankind into an exclusive feature of Arab national life. The various puritanical religious movements whose sole objective has been the restoration of Islam to its former purity and simplicity, from the Wahhabis of Najd to the populist movements of the 1980s, are interpreted by the nationalists as an essential part of the Arab national consciousness.

The national sentiment in the Arab East started and remained an eclectic composition. European encroachment and Ottoman decline led to the political subjugation of several parts of the Muslim lands and peoples and virtual political rule was extended to the Arab lands during the First World War. The spread of European domination was accompanied by an attitude of patronizing superiority towards Islam among its public figures which spread to become universally accepted. In particular, the nineteenth-century activist Jamal al-din al-Afghani had a public controversy with the French scholar Ernest Renan which hardened French and Arab attitudes to each other. Muslims were portrayed as backward, primitive and barbaric. The reaction was strong and at times violent. It led the new ideologues to call Muslims to rise up to the European challenge and counter it. A number of them put forward a view of Islam that was distinctly political. Al-Afghani and his many disciples proposed to renovate the solidarity of all Muslims so that they could be transformed into a world power. To them Islam was essentially a political doctrine and only incidentally a faith. The basic demand of religion had become loyalty and not necessarily piety, a sentiment whose reverberations can still be heard throughout the Muslim world.

Needless to say, these contentions run counter to the traditional Muslim view of religion. The Orthodox view is that Muslims are Muslims not because they think that their faith was able to construct a powerful political state in the past and possesses the power to do it again, but because they believe in the Revelation of God to his prophet Muhammad. As such they should build their life in accordance with divine precepts in order to obtain divine blessings in this world and secure salvation in the one to come.

It was a fundamental belief in the sanctity and integrity of the Muslim community and its essential unity that led many of the early nationalists in the Arab East to avoid advocating

Arab independence from the Empire. The Young Turks' revolt in 1908 encouraged them to seek rights for Arabs within the new constitutional framework which the Young Turks introduced into the Ottoman state. Political parties, groups, societies and clubs were formed to promote fraternity between Arabs and Turkey. The Ottoman Decentralization Party, established in Cairo in 1912 by Arabs with experience of public life, attracted many members of the intelligentsia in the Arab East. Secret organizations like al-Qahtaniya, named after the legendary ancestor of the Arabs, Qahtan, advocated the creation of a dual Turkish-Arab Empire, much like the Austro-Hungarian Empire, in which the unity of the peoples was maintained by the separation of their governing institutions. The idea of autonomy for the separate ethnic groups of the dying empire gained increasing popularity and acceptance but it was practically too late to undertake such major changes.

Despite the formation of these groups and the sentiments they expressed, the Arabs had a powerful motive not to demand secession: the fear of complete disintegration of the Muslim political community, which was to them a cardinal feature of the Islamic way of life. It was obedience to their religion that led them to continue the association with their co-religionists, the Turks. But when the Turkish leaders of the ruling Union and Progress Committee (CUP), the Young Turks, showed their hand, particularly after the putsch of 1909 when the Sultan attempted to overturn their rule, a distinct trend away from this association began to emerge. Despite these conflicts in Istanbul, the general direction of Ottoman policy became steadily more and more exclusively Turkish. Positions of power were reserved for Turks and the natural beneficiaries were the Turkish subjects of the Empire. The desire for a Turkish-Arab accommodation began to wither away. The Arabs began to look for ways to justify secession and to face the dangerous consequences of the break-up of the Ottoman Empire, and with it the political community of Islam.

The move had to be justified on two separate grounds. The first was easy and straightforward. The Arabs and Turks, though both Muslims, had become incompatible communities in the conduct of political affairs. The nationalism of the Young Turks, it may be said, turned their co-religionists into Arab nationalists by default. The aspirations of both were so irreconcilable that the two groups had to go their separate ways. Suppression by the Turks drove many Arabs to embark on clandestine political activities abroad. Arab intellectuals, many of them Syrian Christians rather than Muslims, flocked to Cairo or Paris, where Arab exiles had been active for some years. It is significant that many of these ideologues were Christians, not Muslims. It followed that the main drift of anti-Turkish propaganda was secular, not religious, thus introducing an element of separation between the concept of Arab nationalism and Islam as a religion.

As early as 1904 Najib Azouri in Paris had founded the League of the Arab Fatherland and published a journal called *L'Indépendence Arabe* in 1907. In 1911 Arab refugees there formed the Young Arab Society (*al-Fatah*). The group resolved to reject the idea of any integration within the empire and worked for full Arab freedom and independence. In 1914 the society moved its headquarters to Damascus in Syria. Another organization was the Covenant (*al-Ahad*) whose founder was Aziz Ali al-Misri. Al-Misri later served as Chief of Staff of the Arab armies that raised the banner of the Arab revolt led by the Hashemites against Ottoman rule and for Arab independence.

The second ground for the separation of the Arab provinces of the Empire involved the more difficult argument of religious justification. It was derived from certain notions of the religious reform movement led by Afghani and many of his Arab disciples. In their call for the restoration of Islam to its original purity and simplicity there was the implicit notion that the glorious past of Islam rested with the Arabs above all other Muslims. The underlying assumption was that the deterioration in the power and authority of Islam could be attributed to the dominance of non-Arab elements in the Muslim community. The decline of responsible central government by the Ottomans was thus associated with their usurpation of a position in the Muslim community that

23

legitimately belonged to the Arabs. As the religious, and therefore political élite of the Muslim community, the Arabs must assume the leadership once again in order to safeguard their identity both in religious and national terms.

Thus the regeneration of Islam could only be undertaken by the Arabs, especially those of the peninsula, as they were completely free of association with any faction, political or religious, within the Muslim community. They would have to play a leading role in a Muslim revival comparable with that of the first followers of Muhammad when the Islamic mission began and spread. Although the notion of Muslim unity was still implicit in this interpretation, the objective view of the world of Islam and its division into several states and domains made it possible for the Arabs to draw themselves apart and to seek the establishment of their own distinctive nationhood in the Arabic-speaking world of Islam.

The Arab Revolt and its aftermath

It was the interaction of these factors that brought about the alliance between the nationalist societies and the traditional ruling houses of Arabia. Amongst the latter, the Hashemite family, as direct descendants of the Prophet and hereditary Amirs of Mecca, was the best known and most influential. Sharif Hussein, who led the Arab Revolt a few years later, had been the focus of attention not only for the Arab nationalists and the Ottomans, but also for the European powers. As a precaution against the Sharif leading a rebellion against the rule of the Sultan in the Hijaz (as many of the other Arab potentates, such as the Imam of Yahya in the Yemen and Muhammad al-Idrisi of Asir had done), Sultan Abdul Hamid invited Sharif Hussein to Istanbul. Ostensibly he was an honoured guest. In fact he was a prisoner and a hostage against Shariffian designs and ambitions for the Arab people. However, the Young Turks' revolution brought a fortunate, if accidental, end to his captivity. Sharif Hussein was able to end his exile in Istanbul and return to Mecca to claim his rightful place as guardian of the Muslim holy places in Mecca and Medina and as ruler of the Hijaz. Moreover, the Sharif's sons entered the new Ottoman parliament as representatives for the Arab provinces. The parliament in Istanbul provided a legitimate platform for the expression of political opinion and views and a convenient meeting place for politically conscious Arabs from various parts of the Empire. Parliamentary experience offered the Hashemite princes the opportunity to acquaint themselves with Arab affairs and made them familiar with the Arab political organizations which became so crucial in the planning of the revolt.

The second son of the Sharif (my grandfather and founder of the kingdom of Jordan) was, without doubt, the most dynamic member of the Shariffian household. It was his initiative that made it possible for his father to return to the ancestral home in Mecca. Having contacted members of the Young Turks' junta, he prevailed upon his father to send a telegram to the Sultan claiming the Amirate of Mecca and he himself went to see Kamil Pasha of the Young Turks to force the claim. My grandfather's acumen and foresight set in motion contacts with the British in Cairo in 1914, which eventually culminated in the Hussein–MacMahon correspondence and the Arab Revolt of 1916. The initial overtures made by Abdullah were extremely discreet. He simply indicated that Sharif Hussein was willing, provided certain conditions were met by Britain, to consider leading the movement for Arab independence. Suspicion that the Sharif was harbouring these intentions soon became public knowledge, as the third son of the Sharif, Faisal, began to make similar overtures in nationalist circles and among the secret societies of Arab officers and intellectuals from Syria and Iraq, initially to effect a change in Turkish policy but eventually to seek Arab independence.

The Young Turks acted to suppress the authority of the Sharif in Mecca. A new Amir of Hijaz was appointed, Sharif Ali Haidar, whose task was to destroy Hussein. However, by the spring of 1914 the Turks realized that Sharif Hussein had successfully consolidated his position with the tribes of the Hijaz to forestall this counterattack. The defeat of the Turkish nominee became the first critical sign of Arab defiance against Turkish suzerainty. It was the first in a long series of trials of strength between Arabs and Turks. The initial result, the defeat of Sharif Ali Haidar, was encouraging. The rest of the struggle, however, proved to be an uphill task.

The course of the general conflict of the First World War, and the diplomatic bargaining, promises and political agreements connected with it, determined the destiny and basic characteristics of the Arab states and their politics up to the present day. These events have continued to dominate inter-Arab relations and influence the political outlook of the majority of Arab leaders. They have also remained to plague relations between Arabs and the West with suspicion and doubt, if not a downright sense of betrayal.

As the Ottoman state threw in its lot with the central powers, Britain began to discard its cautious policy to the demise of the Ottoman hegemony and actively sought alliance with Arab leaders in their war against the Turks. It was at this crucial stage that the interests of the Arabs under Shariffian leadership and those of Britain converged. At the same time, Abdullah began his contacts with the British in Cairo to sound the authorities there on possible Arab–British collaboration in the war.

There was considerable alarm in British political circles at the Sultan's call for holy war, Jihad, against the European Allies. They feared it might find widespread response among Muslims in India and in Egypt, both countries dominated by Britain. If the Jihad was to be forestalled, no one was better placed to pre-empt it than the Sharif of Mecca, Guardian of the Holy Places of Islam. In the correspondence that ensued between the Sharif and MacMahon in 1915, the proposal for Arab independence and the territorial dimensions of the Arab domain were clearly stated. Indeed it was based on the plan that the Decentralization, or Arab Federalist, Party had put forward in order to gain Arab autonomy while maintaining the unity of the Ottoman Empire so that the integrity of the Muslim community would not be brought into question. The demand, however, was no longer the decentralization of power but complete independence of the Arab East under Shariffian leadership.

Sir Henry MacMahon, the British High Commissioner in

Cairo, informed the Sharif that Britain was prepared to recognize and support the independence of the Arabs within the territories specified by Hussein. They included all "the Arab-inhabited territories from Mersin and Adana (parts of Turkey today) down to the Persian Gulf". Some reservations were made about Britain's interest in Iraq, which the Sharif acknowledged. Unbeknown, it seems, to both Hussein and MacMahon, the European Allies, specifically Britain, France and Russia, concluded a treaty, generally known as the Sykes-Picot Agreement, while the correspondence between Cairo and Mecca was proceeding. This treaty undermined and, in some of its provisions, contradicted the understanding reached between the Sharif and the High Commissioner.

The Sykes-Picot Agreement was concluded on 26 April 1916. It allotted Ottoman territories to the three original signatories. Its provisions were not known until the Russians denounced them in 1917 after the October revolution and gave up their claims. Britain and France, however, did not do so, but continued the struggle for the control and domination of the Arab areas allocated to them. France was granted the coastal strip of Syria running northwards from Tyre to Adana, including Mersin, with an eastern boundary line that ran from Tyre to Aleppo in the north through Damascus, Homs and Hama. These territories became the present states of Syria and Lebanon, except for the district of Iskandarun, which France ceded to Turkey in 1938. Britain was allocated territories which became the present-day Iraq, Jordan and the states of the Gulf. Palestine, west of the Jordan from Gaza to Tyre, was designated an international zone, at the insistence of the Russians, because of the Holy Places and the numerous Russian Orthodox institutions there.

However, unbeknown to her partners and certainly without consulting her Arab allies, Britain was to complicate the political future of the Arab East still further by yet another pledge, this time to the Zionist Jews of Europe. Although the Zionist organizations wanted an Allied commitment, only Britain obliged, after a great deal of pressure exerted in the press and on public figures in key positions. On 2 November 1917, A. J. Balfour, Britain's Foreign Secretary, addressed a letter to Lord Rothschild, who represented a number of Zionist organizations. The notorious letter became known as the Balfour Declaration:

His Majesty's Government view with favour the establishment in Palestine of a national home for the Jewish people and will use their best endeavours to facilitate the achievement of that objective, it being clearly understood that nothing shall be done which may prejudice the civil and religious rights of existing non-Jewish communities in Palestine or the rights and political status enjoyed by Jews in any other country.

To go back on pledges made to the Sharif about the future political status of the Arab East was tolerable compared with the granting of a country to a different people – a people who did not reside in it and could not control it. Britain obviously put her immediate military needs and long-term imperial interests before her commitment to the Arabs. The object of this many-faced and contradictory policy was to conciliate Jewish influence in Europe and the Arab support vital in the Near East, while simultaneously preparing the ground for future control of the Arab East to safeguard Egypt and the Suez Canal, Britain's vital link with India.

In order to defuse mounting Arab resentment, and as a means of rectifying this situation, an Anglo-French declaration was made upon the fall of Jerusalem and Baghdad to British forces. In the event, it amounted to no more than another broken promise. It was announced that no future settlement in the Arab East would be made except with the consent of the local populations. This was interpreted by the Arabs as an admission of the right of national self-determination, since it foreshadowed the broad concepts of the American President Woodrow Wilson's fourteen points. Point 12 of the Wilson programme made it clear that the Turkish parts of the Ottoman Empire should have a "secure sovereignty" and that other nationalities would be given "an undoubted security of life and an absolute unmolested opportunity of development". Sharif Hussein, his sons and supporters believed that Wilson's declaration recognized their own national aspirations as submitted and agreed upon in the correspondence with MacMahon. They believed that the fourteen points nullified the Balfour Declaration and all other secret treaties, agreements, commitments, understandings and pledges made under the constraints of total war. Events proved them wrong.

The Sharif and his sons held sway over the Hijaz and the interior of Arabia, including Damascus. Faisal had already been pronounced King of Syria while Abdullah was expected to become King of Iraq. Had the British allowed matters to take their normal course, in accordance with the provisions of the Anglo-French declaration of 1918, there could have been little doubt of the outcome. Self-determination would have led to the confirmation of Faisal in Damascus and Abdullah in Baghdad, if British imperial interests had not stood in the way.

At the Paris Peace Conference, Faisal was entrusted with the Arab case. Lloyd George, the British Premier, went into the Conference assuring the Arabs that they would obtain their legitimate rights. He spoke of their welfare and national aspirations, while pressing the interest, for power and territorial possession, of British imperialism. Egypt, Iraq, Arabia, Palestine, Iran, Cyprus and the Caucasus were all considered British zones of influence, from which the other powers would be excluded and which the local peoples would have to acknowledge. As the American President, Wilson, fell gravely ill, and as most of the territories being negotiated were in the hands of the British military, it was practically Britain alone that decided the fate and destiny of the Arab countries.

In 1920 the San Remo Agreement was drawn up. The major casualty, amongst many, of the contradictory promises made during the war was the abandonment of the pledges made to the Arabs. The provisions of San Remo followed broadly the outline set out in the Sykes-Picot Accord of 1916. The commitment made to the Zionists in the Balfour Declaration was to be honoured. The agreement provided for a Mandatory system of government. It awarded the Mandate over Iraq, Jordan and Palestine to Britain, and that over Syria and Lebanon to France. The Sharif's claim to be King of the Arabs was frowned upon, while other Arab potentates were encouraged to challenge the position. It was clear from San Remo that Britain had resolved her difficulties and problems with her allies, European and Arab, at the cost of the Sharif and his supporters and their political expectations for Arab independence and unity. The only solace the Mandatory system could offer the Arabs was contained in Article 22 of the League of Nations Covenant which stated that the Mandate holding power would extend aid to and advise the Mandated territories when they were fit for statehood.

As the European powers deliberated on the future of the Arab East, the people of the region knew exactly what they wanted. The news of the failure of the Faisal mission to the peace conference did not dampen their spirit. Moves to stifle their national aspirations for unity and independence undertaken by the Allies, such as the separation of Palestine from the rest of Syria and the replacement of British troops by the French under the command of General Gouraud in Beirut and along the Syrian littoral, though ominous, were shrugged off. The General Syrian Congress, composed of eighty-five member representatives from all parts of Syria, including Palestine, met in Damascus in July 1919 and, after considerable free discussion, passed resolutions that defined Arab aims once again. The resolutions called for the independence of Syria, including Palestine, with Faisal as King. A similar but informal Iraqi congress met in the Syrian capital and demanded independence for Iraq with Abdullah as King. Both congresses called for the repudiation of the Sykes-Picot Agreement and the Balfour Declaration, and the rejection of the Mandate. Obtaining no response from the Allies, the Arabs resolved to defy them. In Syria there was a unilateral declaration of independence which France refused to recognize. Military operations were undertaken to drive Faisal's government out of Damascus in 1920. In Iraq there was armed insurrection which British forces had to put down. In Arabia the disagreement between the Allies and the Sharif arising from the conflict between the Sykes-Picot Agreement and the MacMahon correspondence encouraged Abdul Aziz Ibn Saud, ruler of the Nejd, to maintain and strengthen his campaign against the leaders of the Arab Revolt. A march led by Abdullah towards Syria to restore Hashemite rule was under way. Palestine, a country given as a gift to an alien people by an alien power before either could set foot in it, was, and has remained, in turmoil.

The violent reaction of the Arabs to the final outcome of the First World War was the consequence of shattered hopes and unfulfilled expectations. The Arabs felt themselves betrayed. Their predicament has been justly summed up:

To be subjected to foreign occupation, domination, supervision and control and to witness the dismemberment of their homeland by an enemy in the course of a defensive war against an invader was a harsh but predictable fate: to suffer the same fate at the hands of an ally at the conclusion of a successful war was incomprehensible to the Arabs.

They thus had all the more reason to feel disoriented by the breach of the trust they had placed in the West. Their failure to achieve their primary objectives determined the nature of the Arab nationalist movement from then on to the present. Its salient features have been the demand for complete independence and the political unity of the Arab people.

It was perhaps naïve to conclude, as many Arabs had done, that foreign domination was the main reason for their disunity; that the infringement of their independence was the cause and their division the effect. If this had been the case, it would have followed that the removal of foreign denomination would leave the Arabs free to recover their unity. But this has not proved the case.

The impact of Zionism

Once the Arab states became separate political entities, they developed a sense of their own national interest. The local political leaders gained confidence in their administration and the people became accustomed to living within the confines of the new national boundaries. The older and more fundamental concept of Arab independence and unity was overshadowed by new forms of association derived from current political realities. These took shape in the form of the

League of Arab States, set up in 1945. The League, though conceived as the first step towards the long-desired unity, has so far proved more of an obstacle than a help towards the purpose for which it was founded. It recognized the member states as sovereign entities and undertook the task of protecting their territorial integrity. Rivalries and disputes between and among Arab states made this new dispensation acceptable, although most Arabs remain opposed to it. It has been a paradoxical feature of inter-Arab politics that the further the concept of unity slips away, the greater Arab attachment to it becomes.

In the period between the two World Wars the idea of nationalism and radical political action became the vogue under the impact of fresh European political ideologies. The examples of Germany and Italy left a mark on the new generation of Arab nationalists. It was in this period that the more prominent Arab writers and thinkers, who, like their pre-war predecessors, were mainly Christian not Muslim, came to seek a new definition of the Arab national identity. They started to explore the determining characteristics of Arab nationhood. They began to enquire whether their nationalism required a philosophy, just as they did in the 1950s and 1960s when the question was raised as to whether Arab nationalism needed a comprehensive programme of political action or ideology. The earlier sense of betrayal led many of them to look towards Germany and Italy as examples to be emulated, just as later Nasser of Egypt and Qasim of Iraq, as well as many others, looked towards the USSR for help and assistance in the reconstruction of the Arab political order.

However, in the literature of the inter-war period there is scarcely a treatise on the form which Arab unity might take, the manner in which it could be brought about, or the means by which it would be accelerated. The political thinkers of the age were much more concerned with theoretical proofs for the existence of the Arab nation rather than blueprints or programmes for the practical implementation of their notions into functioning political structures. Their writings were marked by a single trend, a constant apologia. They were apologetic about their basic demand, thus always on the defensive and therefore always negative. Since they attributed the political fragmentation of the Arab world to the designs and machinations of the European powers, they immediately concluded that the mere attainment of independence would destroy the artificial barriers and remove the obstacles to unity.

The fact that this argument was an over-simplification did not apparently disturb them. They completely under-estimated the disruptive political currents latent in Arab society. No attention was paid to the innate diversity, as well as the sense of community, in the region. The centrifugal forces drawing the Arabs away from unity – rivalry among Arab rulers, the discords of Arab politics, the ingrained individualism and parochialism of the Arab character – failed to impress them. They were so engrossed in their idealistic projections for the future that they could not pause and take note objectively of the realities of their own present situation.

It is no exaggeration to assert that only the Hashemites and their immediate supporters have been completely conscious of this over-simplification and aware of the implicit dangers which threaten Arab society with fragmentation. Nowhere has this been shown more clearly than in the different attitudes to the question of Palestine, which has continued to be a source of conflict and war ever since the Balfour Declaration. While successive British governments wrestled with the irreconcilable provisions of the Declaration, trying to reconcile its pro-Jewish first half, promising to facilitate the establishment of a Jewish national home, with the guarantees made to the Arabs in its second half, it was Faisal who conducted talks with some of the Zionist leaders for a possible accommodation on Jewish settlements in Palestine. However, Faisal made it clear that this would be effective only when the whole of Syria, including Palestine, was pronounced an independent Arab state. The San Remo Agreement put an end to that expectation.

The Hashemites did not give up their quest for reconcili-ation when the Holy Land and the city of peace, Jerusalem, became a land of blood and violence. Throughout the period of the Mandate, King Abdullah tried to convince both Jews and Arabs that they could live together in peace and harmony. Both Abdullah and Nuri al-Said of Iraq intervened energetically to stem the violence which characterized the 1930s by urging both Jews and Arabs that co-existence was still possible. Both men were true to the original Shariffian aims of simultaneously seeking the independence and unity of the Arab East.

The main features of the history of the Palestine question are now all too familiar. To put it bluntly, the Palestinians witnessed the hijacking of a whole country – their own – and found themselves expected to acquiesce and approve. They did not. No one should have expected them to do so; indeed there was no good reason why they should submit to the giving away of their country. Palestinians could not understand how it could be supposed that the importation of an alien people, a people that sought to become the majority in the country within a few years, would not automatically "prejudice the civil and religious rights of the existing non-Jewish Arab communities in Palestine", as the Balfour Declaration had put it. They interpreted British policy as active complicity with Zionist aims. The purpose of both, as they saw it, was the colonization of Palestine, the inevitable consequence of the Declaration. Winston Churchill, speaking in the House of Commons on 14 June 1921, expressed the dilemma facing Britain in these succinct terms:

The difficulty about the promise of a National Home for the Jews in Palestine is that it conflicts with our regular policy of consulting the wishes of the people in the Mandated territories and of giving them representative institutions as soon as they are fitted for them, which institutions, in this case, they would use in order to veto any further Jewish immigration.

Zionism as a national ideology for the Jews started in central Europe with the single aim of colonizing Palestine. It thus began as a nationalism without a country or a land of its own. Palestine was neither a virgin nor a vacant land. The Zionists became nationalists of a country they did not inhabit or control. Yet they claimed it to be their fatherland. The first instrument of nation-building for Zionism was not the struggle for independence and the establishment of nationhood in a land already inhabited by Jews, but a gathering in, a reversal of the diaspora in the colonization of Palestine. The aim of Zionism, in the words of the Jewish historian Israel Cohen, "is to create for the Jewish people a home in Palestine secured by public law". The Balfour Declaration did just that. What was a convenience for the British and a triumph for the Zionist Jews was a disaster for the Arabs, since Palestine belonged only to them, its original inhabitants who refused to give it up. In this lay the source of the dilemma faced by successive British governments and which King Abdullah of Jordan, my grandfather, amongst others tried to resolve.

The sinister consequences of the colonization of Palestine by the Zionists had become all too clear very early on. Unlike other European settlers and colonizers – the British in India, the French in North Africa and the Dutch in South East Asia – the Jews did not flock to Palestine for economic or strategic reasons – trade or the protection of trade routes – but to attain nationhood for themselves. Another basic difference from earlier European settlers was the fact that the Zionists did not want to live or co-exist with the indigenous population of Palestine, the Arabs. The Palestine Arabs had to go, since the Zionists could not expect Jewish immigration on a scale that would make them a majority in the land (their prerequisite for nationhood) if they remained. The Arab inhabitants, as they continued to live and work on the land of their forefathers, became an obstacle that had to be removed. A third major difference from European settlers elsewhere in the world was that the Zionists could not rely on the resources and strength of their own "home" governments to maintain their position. They had to create their own apparatus to enable them to do so; a local army and a police force became the means to their survival and the instrument of state-making.

Arab resistance to Zionist policy as it unfolded itself in their country soon flared up into riots. Violent demonstrations, an open rebellion, in 1920, 1921 and again in 1929, culminated in 1936 in the Arab uprising which was sustained until 1939.

The violence in Palestine prompted the British government to despatch a Royal Commission – the Peel Commission – to investigate the situation and make recommendions for a settlement. In 1937 the Commission reported its findings.

It produced an unexpected conclusion, but one that had, in the light of events in Palestine in the preceding twenty years, become inevitable. There was, it found, an irreconcilable conflict between the aspirations of the Arabs and the Zionists. These aspirations could not be satisfied under the terms of the Mandate. Partition was therefore the only way out of the dilemma in which Britain found herself. The small country of Palestine was to be divided into three zones: a Jewish state comprising one-fifth of the Mandated territory, including most of the seaboard; an Arab state mainly situated in the central plateau; and a British zone for Jerusalem and its environs. The original policy of fostering a bi-national state was deemed to have failed.

The Palestine Arabs rejected the recommendations of the Peel Commission, just as ten years and another World War later they turned down the UN partition plan. In 1947, when the clash of national aspirations and political demands was intensified, Britain turned the Palestine problem over to the newly established United Nations. The United Nations set up a Special Committee on Palestine – UNSCOP – to do what the Peel Commission had failed to do ten years earlier. The report on its findings led inescapably to the same conclusion – partition. UNSCOP simply substituted a UN-administered zone in Jerusalem for the Peel Commission British zone.

There were good reasons why the partition plan should have outraged the Arabs. First, they questioned the right of anyone else, whether Britain or the United Nations, to partition their country without consultation. Apart from this point of principle, the partition scheme sought to include within the Zionist state all areas owned and inhabited by Jews, even though this meant the inclusion of large parts of the country owned and inhabited by Arabs. In fact, in the section allotted to the Jews 50 per cent of the population were Arabs, while the Jews owned less than 10 per cent of the land. The Arab sector, on the other hand, was to include the smallest proportion of Jewish property and fewer than 10,000 Jewish residents. The disparities glaringly favoured the Zionists who, in view of their determination to set up an exclusively Jewish state, were bound to force the Arabs to abandon their homes and property in the Jewish sector. The call for Arab national self-determination went up and the campaign has remained vigorous ever since: it has been the cause of five major outbreaks of violence between Arabs and Zionists, in 1948, 1956, 1967, 1973 and 1982.

The Zionist quest to control and dominate the whole of Palestine, irrespective of its tragic consequences for the country, must be contrasted with the Arab willingness to contemplate a sizeable Jewish presence in the country protected by every provision necessary to ensure its survival. King Abdullah made several attempts throughout the period of the Mandate. However, following the inconclusive London Round Table Conference which Britain called to compose Arab–Jewish differences in 1939, Abdullah made public his plan for the unity of Transjordan and Palestine, which provided for an autonomous administration for the Jews in the country. The territorial limits of the autonomous region were to be decided by a joint commission made up of Arabs, British and Jews. The Jews were to have representatives in a parliament whose members would have been drawn from both communities. The plan conceded the contentious issue of Jewish emigration to Palestine, but called for its regulation and direction. Some three years later, when moves to establish the Arab League were set in motion by Nuri al-Said of Iraq, the same provision made for the Jews in the Abdullah plan was repeated and extended to include the Christians of Lebanon in a greater union of Syria linked with Iraq in a confederacy.

It was typical of the foresight of the Shariffian leadership to consider the problem of the minorities which has become such a burning issue in the 1980s. Imbued with the higher Islamic sense of justice and tolerance, the Hashemites, whether in Arabia, Syria, Iraq or Jordan, have made energetic efforts to ensure the security as well as the orderly integration of the religious and ethnic minorities in the political process of the countries they governed. Faisal had shown the way in Damascus when he was welcomed by the Christian leaders of the country as their sovereign. In Iraq the principle was put into effect in an institutionalized manner. The electoral law of Iraq specified that Christians and Jews would have their own members of Parliament elected in the major cities of Baghdad, Mosul and Basra. In the first cabinet formed in Iraq the Minister of Finance was a prominent Iraqi Jew, who continued to serve in the same capacity for several years and under different premiers until developments in Palestine made it difficult for him to continue in the post. Faisal was so concerned that his removal might be interpreted as a move to exclude members of the minorities from the process of government that he had a well-known Christian public figure appointed in his place.

It is significant that these events took place in the 1920s and 1930s. But no further progress has been made towards greater national integration in politics; instead, the process has been reversed since the mid-1930s. The early constructive moves were first obstructed and then cut off by the contagious growth of extremist politics. The concept of national exclusiveness advocated by the ultra-radical wing of the Zionist movement intensified and polarized political aspirations based on ethnic and religious differences. About fifty years later the same advocates are no longer wanted men but the rulers of the country they coveted with vengeful violence. At the same time, their cause has served as a catalyst for the emergence of a similar breed of men on the Arab side. It is all too evident that people have learnt the wrong lesson. Violence and war, it seems, do pay. We must at all costs re-establish and maintain the middle ground for peace and reconciliation or we will all perish in a perpetual cycle of conflict. Arab traditional values and aims must be restated and redefined. A fresh confirmation of our beliefs is required so that the Arab march towards a better future is clearly marked and signposted.

2 The Arab Political Process

The desire among contemporary Arabs to experiment with political modernization is directly related to the adoption of West European norms and methods of government. Many young educated Arabs, including members of my Hashemite family, have tended to look towards Europe with admiration. They have sought inspiration, not just a model, for the reform and adaption of their traditional system of government in order to meet the needs and requirements of the modern age. The Arabs expected encouragement, intellectual generosity and fair treatment in their quest to find a modern political system. They have been disappointed in all three and, in turn, their attitude towards the West has been overwhelmed by a sense of disbelief and disillusionment. The terms of the settlement after the First World War were a shattering blow to their hopes and aspirations. The growth of a mutual understanding was brusquely halted, and the old ambivalence which characterized the relationship between Islam and the Arabs on the one hand, and the West on the other, began to harden.

Ever since then, the Arab political process has become obsessed by two features of the post-war settlement: the division of Arab lands into arbitrary "zones of influence" and "Mandated territories", which gave rise to the present state system; and the imposition of Western control under the pretext of "supervision" and "guidance". These were seen as an integral part of the terms agreed upon in Paris, which were particularly offensive since they were drawn up not in accordance with pledges and undertakings made to the Arabs, but to satisfy the interests of the Western allies and to settle disputes amongst them. The Arab reaction was a call for the immediate unity and complete independence of the Arab East. The sense of grievance against the post-war settlement soon led the new generation of Arabs to reject all vestiges of Western influence, including any adoption of Western political institutions. It was further embittered as the struggle for Arab unity and independence against West European states became more overt and active. The need to get rid of these twin restrictions on their liberty dominated the development of a national movement to the exclusion of everything else. The dominance of these features in the politics of the Arab East has undoubtedly hampered the evolution of a sound political process based on a representative system. It has also hindered the development of fresh civic norms of behaviour which would have led to the formation of proper and functioning public institutions.

In the building of a nation, the purpose of Islam is not simply to exhort the faithful to do good and avoid evil, but to construct a perfect and righteous society – a community in which the Divine Laws of God will prevail. Islam, as such, knows no distinction between a religious and a temporal realm. There can be no differentiation between state and church, since there is no church in Islam. The state is, in theory at least, an integral part of the religious law. Both religion and politics – the spiritual and secular dimensions of the state – form a unity under the all-embracing laws of *al-Sharia*. Thus, the Islamic concept of the state is that of a perfect and immutable entity within the Islamic tradition.

Under this generally acknowledged dispensation, the individual Muslim, Arab or otherwise, is confronted with an important obstacle in the evolution of certain political notions. The obstacle, however, is more apparent than real. Traditionally, Muslims have been unable to study politics as a completely separate discipline from the traditional approach to religious jurisprudence. Because of this, vital problems arose concerning the nature of the state, the concepts of authority and power, the variety of government institutions, the attributes and qualifications of rule and the limitations on the use of power, which have not been felt to need a comprehensive or decisive situation. Despite the gradual adoption of civil codes, these beliefs, as well as others, such as individual rights and obligations, could not be examined and assessed except within the jealously guarded laws of Islamic jurisprudence. The nationalist struggle had cast such a dark shadow that modern Arabs had little time and no intellectual will to tackle these fundamental problems.

The restrictions imposed by centuries of history became the accepted norm. Rigidity, inherited and venerated, created an interminable dilemma. The individual Muslim was confronted with his religion's demand for the establishment of a just and righteous administration, while at the same time he felt unable to impugn the validity of a system of government rooted in orthodoxy and ordained by the religious laws. This was particularly difficult as the state could not be conceived to exist except in religious terms. Obedience to the central authority of the ruler was a religious obligation and defiance was tantamount to a rejection of the Muslim order and therefore heresy. Clearly, defiance of a Muslim ruler was seen as the negation of accepted tradition, so that any established order was preferable to none, provided it conformed to religious laws.

This interpretation of the religious law governing Muslim administrative practices has resulted in an unacceptable degree of constraint in the conduct of public affairs. The problem was further exacerbated by the absence of a coherent religious formula for political action which would have provided the essential guidelines for future Islamic governance. The whole arrangement had to rest on the exhortations in *al-Sharia* to the ruler to be just, righteous and magnanimous for his own good and to fulfil his Islamic obligations. The lack of an institutional framework to supervise, check and control the performance of the ruler meant that the only sanction upon him was his own fear of God.

Over the centuries, the conflict between spiritual and temporal demands intensified, and the *Ulema*, the assembly of religious teachers and jurists, who initially assigned to themselves the significant role of guardians of the correct application of religious laws, became subject to the political manipulation of rulers. Occasionally they were prevailed upon to provide religious sanction of a political order of questionable legitimacy. More often than not they obliged, mainly because of their concern for the well-being and the integrity of the Muslim community. Their objective was to preserve the unity of that community, their fear lest it should break down. In many cases it became obvious that the very people who were charged with the task of protecting and upholding strict Muslim values, the guardians of the validity of the Muslim system, had become the mainstay of its abuse.

It was this political legacy with which Arab modernizing rulers and religious reformers had had to contend since the beginnings of the nineteenth century. Many of them came to the conclusion that, in the absence of a divine formula for government embodied in an institutional framework which could truly be regarded as Islamic, they could chart their own way and devise their own modes of government. It was at this juncture that modern European ideas and concepts began to make an impact on Muslim societies in the East. Until then, and despite the vicissitudes of Muslim rulers, traditional Islam continued to view European Christendom as a political rival and an enemy of Muslim doctrine and power. Muslims were apt to dismiss European civilization as something incomplete, superseded, and above all, irreligious. Their attitude was essentially derived from the absolute conviction of the irrefutable superiority of their own way of life and the validity of their faith as the last of the divine messages to mankind.

This settled view was suddenly shattered by the decline in Muslim power and the emergence of strong and powerful nations in Europe. A period of readjustment followed, culminating in the wholesale adoption of many European concepts and methods of government. The introduction of these reforms within the Ottoman Empire became known as the *tanzimat* movement or *nizami jadid*, the "Reorganization" and the "New Order" respectively. Considerable care had to be taken to justify and explain the introduction of measures to reorganize the armed forces, government, education, health and transport. But above all, changes in the laws governing the status of the individual had to be made on religious grounds, if they were not to be condemned as innovations and therefore unacceptable to Islam because of their violation of basic Muslim tenets. It was around the 1850s, for instance, that Muslims and non-Muslims were declared to be equal before the law. Both were called upon to bear arms in defence not just of the community but of the territorial state as well.

Most Muslim communities, faced as they were with the threat of European domination, decided to emulate the West so that Western penetration of the Islamic world might be checked. At the outset, they sought the importation of Western weapons, military organization and industrial technique. A direct consequence of this movement was the secularization of government institutions, which was seen as the essence of European civilization. The purpose was to infuse into the Muslim way of life what it so clearly lacked – constitutional government, freedom of political thought and parliamentary democracy.

Nonetheless, the movement towards cultural borrowing was marked by an inevitable ambivalence in the relationship between Muslims and European culture and civilization. While admiring European power and technology, the individual Muslim resisted alien domination, and resented his own weakness and the frailty of the civic institutions which had necessitated the process of emulation. This resentment, compounded by European political domination and aggravated by its tendency to denigrate and belittle the Islamic cultural heritage, was manifested in violent reactions against the West, and was conveniently labelled in European circles as Muslim xenophobia. The dialectics of this relationship contributed in no small measure to the revivalist movement, generally characterized today as Muslim fundamentalism and Islamic militancy.

The further problem that obstructed the efforts of the religious reformers was the difficulty of developing secular political theories out of their religion. This was particularly hard since Islam is distinguished from other religions by virtue of being a sacred juridical system. The result is that political thoughts and concepts in Muslim countries are derived from European philosophic and political traditions, although they are applied in a Muslim context and with an Islamic content. They are concerned mainly with two issues which have been formulated in European terms: the quest for political independence coupled with the establishment of a sovereign state on the one hand, and, on the other, the search for determinants of the nature and limits of government. In this process, the reformers have had to rely not so much on the letter of inherited wisdom but on the spirit and essence of Islamic doctrine. Pursuing this major, if long-neglected, principle of interpretation, Muslims were able to chart the way for their own future and determine the nature of state and government. They came to the conclusion that there was no fundamental incompatability between the concept of the nation-state and Islam, or between Islam and the principles of constitutional government.

The introduction of these new modes of political thought and conduct within the Ottoman Empire was sanctioned by the religious authorities so as to ensure their compatibility with the fundamental tenets of Islam, evidence of the continuing need to balance the need of government with the Divine Law. Religious leaders of different schools and from various parts of the Muslim world became engaged in an effort whose primary function was to examine the state of their religion and the position of the community of believers in the contemporary world.

They conceded that through internal weakness and error, as well as external pressure and influence, Islamic values and standards had been distorted and corrupted. Their conclusion was that true Islam, a dynamic, humane, liberal and living religion, must be rejuvenated and defended if the Muslims were ever to withstand Western attacks and survive Western competition. This movement has resulted in two divergent schools of thought. There was, on the one hand, the school of liberalism, which called for the establishment of a modern Westernized system of government and society, and, on the other, the fundamentalist school, which has sought to remould the present in the image of the past.

Throughout the Muslim world, and particularly in the

Middle East, countries like Turkey, Egypt and Iran began a serious attempt to introduce and operate a system of liberal democracy, with written constitutions, elected sovereign legislators, independent judiciaries, political parties and a free press. Soon after the First World War, the countries of the Arab East followed suit, only to have their brave *démarche* frustrated by the provisions of the post-war settlement. The Arabs found their cultivated sense of national integrity shattered by the division of their national domain into states and zones of influence for the purpose of accommodating the strategic interests of their European allies. The shock was even more traumatic when they realized that their aspirations for complete independence were no longer attainable. Under these conditions, the cautious Arab quest for a modern political process no longer concentrated on the system of government, but on the two precepts that initially determined the nature of the Arab national struggle: Arab independence and the unity of the Arab homeland.

Today, everywhere in the Arab East, the experiment with the liberal constitutional system of government appears to have failed. Democratic institutions have been abandoned in many of the Arab states in favour of a more totalitarian system of government. In other states of the region, the adaptation of the Western system of government is in such a state of disrepair or collapse that the search for a viable alternative has been active for some years past.

The distrust which has characterized Arab–Western relations began to crystallize gradually. The alliance gave way to a sentiment of betrayal and bad faith at the West's reluctance to honour its pledges to the Arabs. The peace settlement transformed that disillusionment into hostility and outright rejection of whatever the West had to offer. The anti-Western mode of thought was so pervasive that governmental institutions adapted from Western practices were seen as the embodiment of that Western domination which had become only too real and obvious.

The purpose of Western collaboration with the Arabs was no longer perceived as purely for the benefit of the Arabs so that they might gain their independent nationhood, but to serve, first and foremost, the imperial interests of the West. It was a sudden revelation for many of the Arab leaders, including members of my own family, that the West Europeans, and the British in particular, had not ventured to the Arab East to vindicate the emergence of an Arab nation and preserve the political and national integrity of its people. Naïve, I suppose, they were, but they were new and innocent practitioners in the complex and devious game of international statecraft.

What they could not fathom was the importance of the Arab East as a vital strategic area and that British policy was framed to protect its own essential interests: namely, the safety of British imperial lines of communication and the exploitation of the region's rich oil resources. The immediate objects of the policy were to achieve effective domination of the Arab regions and populations, and to attempt to organize them so as to ensure permanent possession or influence. Usually this was done through the manipulation of a combination of financial, economic and military sanctions. The noted historian of the Near East, and my erstwhile mentor at Oxford, Albert Hourani, has put it another way. He did not believe that foreign control was established for the sake of the inhabitants of the Arab countries or of the territories that they occupied. It was brought about as an incident in the European nations' struggle for the domination of other strategically or economically important regions of the world. They occupied the Middle East in order to go somewhere else, or to prevent their rivals doing so. Their interests in the region stemmed from the desire to obtain or to create outlets for surplus production; once the exploitation of oil became important, they went to the area to obtain it, or prevent their rivals from obtaining it. He continues: "What was important for them was the land and its resources. Those who happened to occupy the land were at best instruments for – at worst, obstacles in the way of – purposes which were no concern of theirs." This attitude was overtly expressed when a British observer referred to the Arab territories after the First World War as constituting "the first brown dominion, not the last brown colony". At present, the method is different but the purpose appears to be the same in determining the approach and policy of the two superpowers, the United States and the Soviet Union.

To pursue a policy based on the strategic importance of an area and to ignore its people is always dangerous: in this case it was to have large and unexpected ramifications both for the West and for the Arabs. The problem was compounded when the independence movement began to gather strength and momentum. British and French officials, who were implanted in every department of the new governments to take on the role of the benevolent supervisors, generally persisted in regarding it as the immature projection of adolescent intellectuals, or the work of fanatical agitators who were fighting the wars of yesteryear.

The trouble was that the Arabs were not only denied their unity, but they soon found that their independence was illusory too. Britain had ruled India for two centuries and (more relevantly to the Arab East) Egypt since 1882; despite, or rather because of, this experience, British officials succeeded in devising a system of government through which they practised what the well-known authority on the history of the region, Bernard Lewis, has described as "interference without responsibility".

It was a well-established pattern, which Lord Cromer had put to good use in Egypt when Consul-General in Cairo immediately after the British occupation in 1882. In order to control and supervise government administration in Egypt, Cromer planted advisers in every government office. The system worked well in the initial stages, until the Egyptian nationalist movement regained its confidence a few years after the disastrous Urabi revolt. Cromer and his advisers became the real, but unproclaimed, arbiters over an administrative area of fluctuating dimensions. The effectiveness of their position was dependent on the acquiescence of the Egyptians. However, when the Egyptians began to express their reluctance to co-operate, as they were encouraged to do by Khedive Abbas Helmi II, the whole administrative edifice began to crack and collapse.

Cromer's method of administrative supervision was

47

characterized as that of the "hidden hands" (*al-ayadi al khafyya*), which became the common epithet of the independence movement of the Arab East. The expression acquired a special force when Cromer admitted that the pattern he had set up had worked well because under Tawfiq, Abbas's predecessor, he could remain "hidden" while pulling the "strings" of public administration. Like Abbas Helmi II, the leaders of the independence movement in the Arab East became reluctant to act as puppets on the strings of the British and French High Commissioners and political residents, who were only too keen to take charge of their reluctant wards in the newly designated states of Iraq, Syria, Lebanon and Jordan, and those states that came into existence later. They gradually began to resent and reject this kind of manipulation.

In many instances, the advice proffered by the European High Commissioners and their advisers became synonymous with command. The arrangement infuriated Arab political sentiment and susceptibility. The demand for complete independence became a cardinal feature of national politics. Under this pressure, the concessions made by the Mandatory powers to the nationalists took a distorted form. They served only to heighten tensions between the Arabs and their former European allies.

The concessions were codified in treaties concluded between the Mandatory powers and their wayward charges. The treaties were designed to reconcile two incompatible demands. On the one hand, there was the wish of the Mandatory powers to maintain their position of influence and to protect their interest in the region; on the other, there was the desire of the people of the region to achieve complete independence and the evacuation of foreign troops from their territory.

The conclusion of treaties was conceived by both sides at the time as a practical compromise urged and welcomed by the powers but only tolerated by the Arabs as a transition to complete independence. To all intents and purposes, the treaty relationship between the Arab states and the Mandatory powers offered formal independence which was soon seen to be a mere façade, behind which Cromer's unseen hands pulled the strings and continued to take all the important decisions. Moreover, the concessions made by the Arab states included the right to set up military bases and the acknowledgement of a privileged position for the European powers in the management of national economies and the direction and volume of trade. Such treaties were concluded between Britain and Iraq in 1930, Egypt in 1936, Jordan in 1946, and between France and Syria and Lebanon in 1936, although the latter were never ratified by the French government. Palestine never had the opportunity to negotiate such a treaty with the Mandatory power.

The ostensible purpose of the treaties was to declare these countries independent and to maintain them as equal and friendly allies of the European powers. Meanwhile, the Europeans were enabled to pursue their imperial interests unimpeded, despite the continuing nationalist agitation. In short, the Arab states were granted full self-government in domestic affairs: but, while they enjoyed apparent external sovereignty, they were kept within actual or potential spheres of imperial political power in which bases were set up for operations in defence of imperial interests.

A brief examination of the mechanics of negotiations and the methods of ratification of these treaties indicates the extent of the abuse to which the new parliamentary systems were subjected. The irony was that the liberal constitutional system of government was one of the constructive measures which the Mandatory administrations introduced in most of these countries. Worse still, the new arrangement showed that little change had occurred in the nature of the relationship between the former Mandatory power and its ward. The European power remained the dominant partner in the new system of alliance. Moreover, enormous pressures were exerted to make new sovereign parliamentary bodies submit to the treaty relationship. The alternative to a treaty was made clear. It would not be complete independence as desired by, and promised to, the Arabs, but total subjugation. The inescapable result was a general Arab disenchantment with the West and the vitiation, from the start, of the constitutional parliamentary system of government borrowed and adapted from the Western European model.

For instance, in Iraq, which was the first Arab state to become independent, but which was bound by a treaty relation with Britain, the lengthy negotiations lasted a decade and included a series of treaties, culminating in that of 1930 which conceded the right of formal independence. In 1924 the first constituent assembly was elected only after the mass arrest and deportation of all members of the opposition. Once the elections – manipulated as they were – were completed, the assembly was empowered to do two things: to ratify the first treaty of 1922 and to approve the liberal constitution by which Iraq would be governed. The treaty was drawn up as a substitute for the much resented Mandate. It gave rise to a tide of nationalist sentiment, supported by King Faisal I, who had been installed as monarch over the new kingdom a few months earlier.

The reaction of the British High Commissioner in Baghdad was typical. He issued an ultimatum to the Iraqi government and the newly established constituent assembly that either the treaty must be ratified or the new institutions of state would have to face the consequences. Those threatened consequences were only too clear and familiar. King Faisal had had to confront them in his trials and tribulations with the French High Commissioner in Damascus only four years earlier. In the case of Iraq, they would have amounted to the dissolution of the assembly, the dismissal of the cabinet, delay in the introduction of constitutional powers and the reimposition of the Mandate.

Another example was provided in 1924 when the Iraqi government was reluctant to grant oil concessions to a British company, the Iraq Petroleum Company, which replaced the old and defunct company known as the Turkish Petroleum Company. After the First World War, British officials and other representatives in Baghdad, taking advantage of the territorial dispute with Turkey over Mosul, started a whispering campaign to the effect that Britain might find it difficult to resist Turkey's claim to the oil-rich province if the government of Iraq persisted in its rejection of the new oil agreement. Needless to say, the agreement was duly approved.

It took a great deal of manipulation and arm-twisting, and three treaties (those of 1922, 1926 and 1928) before the conclusion of the final one of 1930, which granted Iraq formal independence, to produce what Iraqi journalists – to the British "mere purveyors of public and political opinion" – dubbed the "peculiar situation" (*al-wad' al-shadh*). The situation was indeed very peculiar. The country was granted formal independence under Mandatory constraints: it had a parliament which was not completely sovereign, a constitution whose provisions were not applied, elections that were not free, and ministerial responsibility only under the watchful eyes of British advisers. Iraq had a desperate need for a strong army but could not have conscription; it had a port and a railway network administered by Iraqis but which did not belong to them; there were privileges for foreigners in Iraq but none for Iraqis abroad. There were many other inconsistencies which arose out of a dual system of administrative responsibilities. These conditions were not confined to Iraq; what was true of Iraq was also true of the other Arab states. France's conduct in Syria and Lebanon left a great deal to be desired, both in ignoring the wishes of the indigenous population and in abusing the institutions that the Mandatory power itself helped to introduce in these territories.

The collapse of the liberal constitutional system of government in the Arab East could not be blamed entirely on the selfishness or heavy-handedness of imperial and Mandatory powers. There were other, more crucial, reasons which made it unworkable at the time. The indigenous political leaders had insufficient familiarity and little training, as well as inadequate support, for the task of operating the system. It was, in all practical terms, an alien system transferred ready-made not only from another country but from another civilization. It was imported by Western or Westernized leadership and imposed on states whose societies had not evolved independently into mature political communities. As such, it could not respond adequately to the strains and stresses of Arab society, nor could it reconcile the incompatible demands of a nationalist movement with the interest of an imperial power. The result was, as Bernard Lewis poignantly puts it, "a political order unrelated to the past or present, and profoundly irrelevant to the needs of the future". The system was doomed from the very outset, since it failed to respond to the deeply felt personal needs of the Arabs or satisfy their nationalist demands for independence and unity. Moreover, it was supported only by the backing of a tiny majority of the intelligentsia: the great majority of the people were baffled by the frequent fall and formation of cabinets, the erratic holding of elections, and the premature dissolutions of parliaments. The shame of it all is that the Mandatory powers and their representatives contributed to these abuses as much by their patronizing attitude and questionable conduct towards parliamentary government as by the unwarranted inter-ference that prevented the evolution of a more responsive system, more attuned to Arab tradition. It was their overt and covert activities that eventually led to the radicalization of Arab politics. The outcome became a foregone conclusion: the rejection of the system as an undesirable semblance of unwarranted Western influence. It was part and parcel of the Arabs' endeavour for independence and assertion of their own integrity.

The public manifestation of the estrangement between the new Arab states and the West was the rejection of Western modes of government. The breakdown of the liberal constitu-tional system of government was compounded by the division of the Arab East into distinct but artificial political entities. The division of the Arab East was blamed on the Western powers and their imperialist designs. The Arab failure to come to grips with the real causes of their disunity caused greater frustrations, which in turn were to radicalize the politics of Arab nationalism in the 1930s. The Arab sense of grievance and betrayal was thus susceptible to the expression given to it by extremist political groupings, which took their cue from the aggressive nationalist and totalitarian ideologies of Europe at the time. Leaders of individual Arab states became obsessed with the desire to see their own respective countries occupy the same position as the Prussia of united Germany or the Piedmont of a united Italy.

However, the quest for unity became still more problematic. In essence, it was transformed from a national campaign for the establishment of a nation state, if a pluralist one, to a struggle for the leadership of the Arab world in which various states staked their claim. The contest has invariably been undertaken in the name of Arab unity. And there is little doubt that the idea of unity has been the most compelling in Arab nationalist thought.

The Arabs have always expressed their allegiance to their unity as a nation, entitled to a state of their own from the moment when they began to recognize themselves as different and separate from their co-religionists, the Turks, albeit citizens of the Ottoman state. Their corporate national identity was already beyond question when the Hashemites raised the banner of the Arab revolt in 1916.

The desire for unity acquired a fresh sense of urgency and purpose after the First World War. The Arabs, naturally enough, blamed the European powers for the division of the Arab East when clumsy and illogical boundaries were drawn to separate them, primarily to meet European interests rather than Arab national demands. Although the idea of unity had been accepted by all the Arabs, and none dared renounce or denounce it, the movement had little to show for itself in tangible results. After more than sixty years of blaming the Arab division on imperialist designs and Western diplomatic machinations, the struggle waged by the Arabs for their unity has been constrained by their own internal tensions, which may yet be regarded as an integral part of the legacy of the West in the Arab East. With the possible exception of the short-lived Syrian–Egyptian union, the movement for unity has only produced invective, recriminations and active intervention by some Arab states in the domestic affairs of others.

The efforts of various political leaders in a number of Arab states to promote their own respective country as the Prussia of the Arab world has been often frustrated because no particular Arab state possesses or can command all the means to realize that objective. This has been shown in the repeated attempts over several decades by Iraq, Syria, Jordan and Egypt to merge into a union. Inter-Arab relations have become so dominated by regional, dynastic and ideological differences and rivalries that it has become extremely difficult for any one country to emerge as the clear leader over all others. The tendency of the various contenders to seek support through the formation of rival blocs within the ranks of the Arab states ensures the existence of a permanent opposition.

Though Arabs are inclined to talk and write incessantly about their unity, yet in the literature of Arab nationalism there is scarcely a single treatise analysing the impediments which have prevented the realization of this cherished national goal. The intervention of foreign powers no longer provides a complete explanation, since all the Arab states have successfully rid themselves of such influences after the achievement of complete independence. Nonetheless, Arab nationalist thinkers are still apt to blame the legacy of the European powers as they emphasise and highlight common factors which unite the Arabs: those of language, history, religion and culture. Yet no outline or theory is put forward for the form which Arab unity may take, or the manner by which it may be brought about.

The longing for unity has remained the main motive force, but it has not been translated into a convincing or realistic programme for political action. The case for unity tends to be either too apologetic or else couched in terms of power politics. Most advocates of comprehensive Arab unity continue to be defensive and their approach therefore negative.

The advocates of nationalist ideologies reiterate the adverse effect of European influence, so that a new generation of Arabs is imbued with extreme notions of anti-Western sentiments. They have monotonously asserted that the political fragmentation of the Arab world is to be blamed on the European powers, and that the mere attainment of independence would remove all obstacles and allow the various Arab states to proclaim their unity. The fact that the artificial barriers set up by the Europeans were not removed after the achievement of independence has evidently escaped the notice of the nationalist thinkers and activists. Baffled and disoriented by the resilience of the state structure of the Arab East, they refuse to look into the dynamics of domestic politics for an explanation. They prefer to take the easy option of blaming outside powers and external forces, both Arab and non-Arab.

The culpability of the Western powers is not only an over-simplification: it has become an increasingly peripheral factor in Arab politics. Yet this has been ignored by the activists as completely as they have underestimated the potency of the disruptive political currents within Arab society itself. They have paid no attention to the built-in factors of diversity that co-exist with the general demands for a uniform community in the region. There are several communities within the Arab world whose social or political grievances are a centrifugal force that draws them away from the cause of unity. They are condemned as anti-nationalist – an attitude which has increased their alienation and brought about sharper social and political conflicts. The alienation of these communities has been enhanced by the discordant streaks in the Arab political canvas and the ingrained individualism and parochialism of the Arab character. It has been further reinforced by the failure of the nationalist ideologists to address the problem of the ethnic and religious minorities. Yet Arabism, the cultural tradition common to all Arabs, has remained the cornerstone of nationalistic ideology and its principal attractive force. It is a cause that continues to generate great enthusiasms amongst all Arabs. The nationalists, however, continue to ignore the religious factors implicit in their ideology that have inspired concern, not confidence, among the minorities.

The relationship between Islam and nationalism has been a source of trouble and confusion for both Muslim and non-Muslim Arabs. For the Muslim Arabs it was Islam that created the basis of the Arab nation by uniting the tribes of Arabia under the banner of a new religion. The non-Muslim must ask what part he can have in a nation whose foundation lies in its religion. However, it is nationalism which, with its special view of historic rights, enunciates the right to independent nationhood. Its appeal as a national ideology for the Arabs lies in the idea of a single powerful Arab state comprising the whole of the Arab nation. Islam is essential to this ideal, but the association should not be superficial. For Islam remains a universal doctrine, not one limited to the Arabs: its use as part of the propaganda of national integration and assimilation has been in fact proved counterproductive to the processes that are meant to lead to the emergence of a uniform political community.

The problem has two aspects. The first is that of political identity; the second, the creation of legitimate rule which responds to the needs and aspirations of the people. While nationalism distinguishes between Arabs and non-Arabs, irrespective of their religion, the Islamic distinction is based on Muslims and non-Muslims regardless of their ethnic and social origins. There has been the further difficulty created by the nationalist inclination to associate their doctrine with orthodox Islam to the exclusion of heterodox sects. Thus, the non-Muslim communities, like the Christian Maronites of Lebanon, as well as the heterodox Muslims like the Shiites, have resented the close association between orthodox Islam and Arab nationalist ideology. They see it as an attempt and a device to maintain the supremacy of the orthodox Muslims in the political process. The non-Arab communities of the area, the Kurds and Turcomans of Iraq and Syria or the Circassians of Jordan, have similarly resented the association. They interpret the emphasis placed on the Arabs as an implicit denial of their own political and civic rights.

The problem of identity is aggravated by the question of legitimate rule. The question of legitimacy is bound up with the nature of the state. A rudimentary definition of the state is an entity where a territorially delimited population is in a position to accept a common form of government. The acceptance of that common form of government on the part of the population renders it legitimate. In this context legitimacy is recognized as the universally acknowledged authority of the ruler to decide for the governed. The power of government is derived from its moral right to issue them. There is, of course, a correlation between the moral right to issue commands and for those addressed to feel a moral duty to obey them. As

S. E. Finer puts it, "Authority represents a two-way process: a claim to be obeyed, and a recognition that this claim is morally right. No public recognition of a claim means no authority." A government acquires such an authority when it provides acceptable bases, laws and regulations for the peaceful resolution of all conflicts arising within all segments of its population. Its ultimate sanction is the absolute right to resort to the instrument of coercion. However, the public acknowledgement of the validity of the law must not simply be the result of the recognition of the overwhelming force at the government's disposal, but the product of a moral acceptance to obey its laws as part of the individual's civic duty.

The unresolved dilemma is whether the Arabs as Muslims should continue to express their primary loyalty and identity to the Muslim community and renounce their particularist claim to nationhood, or whether they should adopt a secular doctrine of nationalism in the Kemalist fashion and reject Islam not so much as a faith but as a political doctrine. However, most nationalists in the Arab world today take the view that they must accommodate Islam in their political ideology, but they all seem to put nationalism before Islam. In short, they would have Islam serve the political purposes of nationalism.

The dilemma is further reflected in any attempt to define who or what is an Arab. It is clear today that the unifying factor is not simply one of language, important as it has been. Definition by language would exclude important segments of contemporary Arab society. Neither is nationalist political consciousness sufficient, even if the ideologists of nationalism insist on it as the major qualification. The definition of an Arab must be measured in cultural and ethnic terms, which include Islam as its central event but do not ignore or neglect other aspects of the long history of the region. As such, the definition remains flexible, yet sufficiently distinct.

Although almost all the precursors of the Arab Renaissance Movement, including some of its early martyrs, were Christian Arabs, as are several of its contemporary ideologists, an Arabic-speaking Christian today may choose not to identify himself with Arab nationalism. However, many more would do so enthusiastically. A Kurd or a Turcoman whose mother tongue is not Arabic would be reluctant to describe himself as an Arab, but, as a Muslim, would have no hesitation in accepting citizenship of a Muslim Arab state. Conversely, a Muslim Arab may profess other political loyalties than Arab nationalism, which may make him reluctant to accept the concept and even reject its political formulation.

More recently, this particular aspect of Arab nationalism has acquired greater significance following the radicalization of certain segments and groups within the Arab nationalist movement, mainly as a result of the repeated failure to resolve the question of Palestine, and the increasing popularity of the Muslim fundamentalist approach to the resolution of the crisis of legitimate rule and of political identity. The popularization of new and radical notions of nationalism and socialism, even the concept of totalitarian democracy, are indeed expressed in Islamic cultural idioms, with many quotations from earlier Muslim authorities. Within its own milieu and on its own terms, Islam is bound to triumph over the ideologists' attempt to keep it in second place. The Islamic approach to this feature of the political process requires the establishment of legitimate political institutions in which the rule of law is supreme, thereby striking a balance between civil and *al-Sharia* law so that the average citizen can enjoy his rights and carry out his obligations without fear or prejudice. Only by combining the spirit as well as the letter of the religious law, by accepting the validity of tradition and the requirements of modernity, can the contemporary Arab achieve the objectives of the Arab Revolt and ensure the ideals of the Arab Renaissance.

Notwithstanding the impression of nationalist ideology and its concomitant anti-Western sentiment, the major initiative to unify Arab ranks was made, ironically enough, by Britain in 1941. This was a crucial year in the development of both the Second World War and Arab politics. German and Italian encroachment had made such inroads not only in the Arab world, but in Europe and Africa as well, that Anthony Eden, Britain's Foreign Secretary at the time, became alarmed at the apparent Arab willingness to co-operate with the Axis powers against the Allies. Well aware of the prevalent anti-Western feeling in Arab political circles, he tried to make a positive gesture to the recurrent demand of Arab nationalism in the hope of reversing an increasingly dangerous trend. In a speech made at the Guildhall in London in May 1941, Eden said:

The Arab world has made great strides since the settlement reached at the end of last war, and many Arab thinkers desire for the Arab peoples a greater degree of unity than they now enjoy. In reaching out towards this unity they hope for our support. No such appeal from our friends should go unanswered. It seems to me both natural and right that the cultural and economic ties between the Arab countries, and the political ties too, should be strengthened. His Majesty's Government for their part will give their full support to any scheme that commands general approval.

Great Britain, the imperial power which, in making and then unmaking the Sykes-Picot Agreement, had set in motion the processes that divided the Arab East, set out this time to unite the region. It is unfortunate that such intellectual generosity has not characterized later British or American policies, despite the threat of the dangers that beset the region from within and without. From the beginning of the Cold War, the policy of the Western Alliance became more rigid and less sympathetic. In particular, John Foster Dulles, the American Secretary of State at the time, pursuing his "Northern Tier" policy of confrontation, saw the Muslim world as a shield against Soviet encroachment, thus giving a new twist to the old imperialist strategy which further disturbed the Arab political balance. My grandfather, King Abdullah, continued to think of Arab unity as a more appropriate concept for the containment of subversive communism. He tried very hard to introduce fundamental changes, aimed at defining and strengthening that concept into the charter of the Arab League which was set up a few years after the Eden speech.

The first response to Eden's encouragement came from Hashemite Iraq, where Nuri al-Said, the former officer in the Shariffian army and by then a prominent political leader in his own country, in 1942 put forward proposals for an Arab union, to be achieved in two stages. First, he recommended the formation of a single state, unitary or federal, as might be found more feasible, which should include all the countries of greater or geographical Syria – present-day Syria, Lebanon, Jordan and Palestine. In this state the Christians of Lebanon and the Jews of Palestine would be granted special autonomy. Second, Nuri proposed an Arab League of states, consisting initially of Iraq and the new Syrian state but open to any other state that might wish to join, whether immediately or later on. The League would have a council with the head of one member state as President, elected in a manner acceptable to all. The council would be responsible for defence, foreign affairs, currency, communications, customs and excise and the protection of minority rights.

My grandfather, King Abdullah, backed Nuri's proposals. Both men wanted a more structured, yet federal, union of these territories. Their advocacy of this union clearly indicated the realism and foresight which had characterized the Hashemite approach to the evolution of a sound and representative system of government in a united Arab East. It was based on the premise that evolutionary processes would ultimately bring about the emergence of a properly integrated political community in the Arab East. It also showed that Arab concern was then primarily focused on the northern part of the Arab East: the southern tier – today's Saudi Arabia, the two Yemens, Oman and the other Gulf states – had not undergone the gigantic development of the last few years, and did not command the financial and economic importance that they enjoy today. (In terms of strategy, of course, these areas have always been important in international power politics, but were not involved in these early moves towards unity.) Diverse and divergent interests in the Arab world and in Europe forced fundamental alterations upon the original plans for Arab union. In the course of 1943, the initiative passed from Nuri of Iraq to Nahhas Pasha of Egypt, from Baghdad to Cairo. Egypt's decision to identify herself with the Arab movement of independence and unity was a turning point in the political evolution of the Arab East. It marked the convergence of the different strands of Egyptian and Arab nationalism which have been running parallel to one another for years.

Quite apart from any commitment to Arab political aspirations, Egypt saw certain advantages in her association with the Arab East. She was the natural candidate for a leading role among a group of Arab states which had to defer to her in view of her superiority in size, power and international status. The Arab states were more than eager to welcome Egypt into the Arab fold, despite the consequent difficulty of imbalance in the talks for unity. With this change in the composition of the Arab community of states came a change in the conception of the proposed League.

It soon became clear, as the negotiations between the various Arab parties went on, that the League could not be integrated or centralized as Nuri had envisaged if it were to include not only Egypt, but Saudi Arabia and the Yemens, as well as Iraq and the countries of geographical Syria. The Arabs had to come face to face with some basic truths about the nature of their society and their political process. There were too many rival dynasties, even in countries amongst republican regimes; there were too many individual national policies, too many differences in social structure and standards of political maturity, and therefore no common outlook between the seven candidate countries (now twenty-two) for any close and meaningful union. Only a loose association that did not infringe the political sovereignty of the member states could accommodate them. The Arab League, which finally came into existence in March 1945, proved to be such an organization. It is no wonder that my grandfather described the final outcome of the unity talks among Arab leaders as "a body with too many heads".

From the outset the organization was limited as an effective force; at times it was virtually immobile. It became a body which did less to bring the Arabs together than to perpetuate their divisions, since it assumed acceptance of the separate political entities as sovereign states whose territorial integrity should not be violated. Moreover, the League institutionalized inter-Arab rivalries and became a forum for complaints by the member states against each other. It has, however, had some success in defusing inter-Arab disputes.

It is the League's inability to redefine the meaningless old political boundaries that has caused so much distress to so many Arabs, individually and collectively. It lies at the source of much public controversy about the right approach to comprehensive Arab unity. Various leaders and public figures have advocated that neighbouring Arab states should endeavour to co-ordinate their policies in all fields, as a preliminary measure towards a wider unity. If these notions are translated into practical policies, it is possible to envisage the creation of a union constructed from four separate building blocks. These would be geographically defined with the states of the fertile crescent as one unit, the states of the Arabian peninsula as another and those of the Nile valley and those of the Maghreb constituting the other two blocks.

The League, however, has played a sustained and positive role in the quest for independence both by other Arab states and by non-Arab states in the Third World. But far from achieving political union, it has shown little enthusiasm for the cause, and its repeated failures to tackle the question of Palestine, particularly after the débâcle of 1948, have discredited it. Many theories have been put forward to analyse and explain the causes of the loss of Palestine and the continuing tragedy of the Palestinian people. They all point one way. Only if the League undergoes some radical reform which will redefine its purpose and re-allocate its functions will it become a body capable of creative action in the Arab community of states. Recently my brother, King Hussein, has suggested a minor but fundamental change to the original charter which would make a decision binding by a majority vote rather than the required unanimity as at present.

It is no exaggeration to suggest that the Arab defeat in Palestine in 1948 has left an indelible mark on the Arab political process and stifled its evolution. It became too obsessed with the various ramifications of the Palestine question to be concerned with its own development and improvement in other directions.

The disillusionment and political alienation felt by Arabs

after their failure to resolve the Palestine question on their own terms was universal; it had a shocking and fundamental effect on Arab politics. Within ten years practically all the governing regimes in the Arab East were overthrown by violent means. The practical effect of the radicalization of Arab nationalism was a succession of military *coups*. In 1949 Syria became the first country to experience a military takeover. Within a few weeks the regime was overthrown, mainly because of indecision as to whether Syria should unite with Jordan or Iraq, or remain independent and allied to Egypt and Saudi Arabia. The second *coup* was followed by another, causing yet more instability in the region as a whole. In 1950, the Lebanese Prime Minister, Riyadh al-Sulh – a man whom King Abdullah held in high regard – was murdered while on a visit to Jordan. A year later a tragedy befell the Hashemite family when King Abdullah of Jordan, the man who managed to protect a major portion of Arab Palestine for its Arab inhabitants, was also assassinated in Jerusalem. In 1952, a free officers' association under the command of Colonel Gamal Abdul Nasser forced King Faruq of Egypt to abdicate in favour of his infant son, only as a first step towards abolishing the monarchy in 1953. Iraq and the Sudan had to wait until 1958, when the Hashemite monarchy in Baghdad and the newly independent government in Khartoum were overthrown by revolution. In both states, it was the growth of constitutional government, which the Hashemite family sought to introduce to the Arab East, that suffered most.

By the mid-1950s, the radicalization of Arab politics had gone so far that most of the ideologists of Arab unity began to speak of the adoption of revolutionary action against all the evils, intellectual, economic, social and political, that were rightly or wrongly linked with European influence on Arab society. An evolutionary approach to the development and improvement of the governing institutions was totally rejected. Revolution in this context meant a fundamental change in the traditional Arab social values. A corollary of this change in political attitude and outlook was a shift in the concept of Arab unity. The notion of revolutionary socialism

63

was injected as a political element in the Arab nationalist programme for action. Socialist thought and policies began to overshadow the nationalist hostility to the West. Anti-colonialism remained the rallying cry, but it was increasingly accompanied by an emphasis on radical political notions sponsored mainly by the new regime in Egypt and nationalist groupings such as the Baath Party of Syria.

It has already been pointed out that Arabism as a belief constitutes a great source of social power, a power all too easily dissipated if different leaders use its name for different and conflicting purposes. Moreover, apart from the original movement, which was led by members of the Hashemite family, the Arabs have found it extremely difficult to evolve a common view of Pan-Arab political leadership. As the ideological orientation of the nationalist movement began to shift, reflecting the conflicting interests of various Arab regimes, huge rifts in Arab ranks began to appear.

The adoption of the Arab nationalist cause by the Nasser regime in Egypt had made sufficient impact on Arab politics to make possible the union of Egypt and Syria into the United Arab Republic in February 1958. The union of the two countries allowed Nasser to play a dominant, but not always constructive, role in the region. The rift in Arab ranks became more complex when it was compounded by the overthrow of the Hashemite monarchy in Iraq in July 1958. The emergence of a revolutionary nationalist regime under the control of the military in Baghdad revived the traditional rivalry between Baghdad and Cairo for the leadership of the Arab East.

The contest between two stridently militant anti-Western regimes blurred the convenient distinction of certain Arab states, like Egypt, Syria and Iraq, as "revolutionary states" as opposed to the "reactionary states", Saudi Arabia, Jordan and the Yemen. This distinction was given currency in countries under the rule of military officers, who used it to identify regimes of which they disapproved – hereditary monarchs, oligarchic politicians, wealthy landowners and businessmen, whose interests were allegedly better protected by keeping the Arab world divided. Their presumed reliance on the West was just one aspect of their reactionary outlook.

The dispute between Egypt and Iraq, both revolutionary states, particularly over the question of independence for the state of Kuwait, indicated that the ideological foundations of the division between the so-called "reactionary" and "revolutionary" states was of little significance. It gave way, from time to time, to political exigencies, the interest and convenience of the military rulers. A close examination would reveal the division to be no more than a struggle for the leadership of the Arabs under an ideological guise.

The establishment of the Egyptian–Syrian union in 1958 meant that radical notions of nationalism and revolutionary socialism acquired a particular Pan-Arab significance. It was acquired from the character of the union's principal architects. President Nasser of Egypt and the Baath Party of Syria stamped their own ideological convictions on the new movement. Both had been directly affected by the trauma of Palestine: from it they drew the conclusion that the last vestiges of European domination would have to be removed from the Arab world. Both professed a foreign policy based on the notion of positive neutrality in the power politics between East and West. Both advocated comprehensive Arab unity; and expressed the need for social, political and economic reconstruction under the central direction and active participation of a unified Arab state. Both partners believed that these objectives could be realized by revolutionary political action.

The union marked the end of one era and the beginning of another. It aimed at the introduction of a new political system – a process borrowed and adapted from the Eastern European model. The syndicalized organization was its foundation, the one-party system its means for social and political mobilization, totalitarian rule its objective and the corporate state its result. Some thirty years later, it has become all too obvious that if the Arab adaptation of the Western political system, the liberal constitutional process, has failed, the new formulation has become an oppressive and stifling instrument. As the margins of individual freedom grew narrower, as national economies collapsed and inter-Arab feuds and recriminations grew more frequent and virulent, it became intolerable. This

65

radical trend in Arab politics saw its climax and demise in the Six-Day War of 1967 and the occupation by Israel of more Arab territory than the worst Arab fears could have anticipated.

The intervening years, between 1958 and 1967, constituted a period of continuous strife and waste of Arab resources. The Arabs engaged in sterile argument about what they should do to their enemy, rather than what they could do for themselves. Although there was a pervading sense of triumph after the Suez War in 1956, it lacked any real basis, except perhaps in the ascendency of Nasser's Egypt over other Arab rivals. Even that came to an end when the UAR broke up in 1961, when Syria seceded after a *coup d'état*. For a short time Egypt withdrew from Arab politics. In 1961, Nasser retreated behind a barricade of socialist reconstruction at home. The model that he offered to other Arab states, fellow revolution- aries as well as antagonistic reactionaries, was universally rejected, and its rejection violently denounced by Egypt. Successful *coups* in Baghdad and Damascus in 1963, led by members and sympathizers of the Baath Party, resulted in inconclusive talks on the reconstruction of a tripartite union. Under these conditions the development of a political process to govern Arab society remained dormant. It was constantly held back by the threat of yet another war between Arabs and Israelis over Palestine. By 1963, the Arab East was again confronted by what has become a familiar pattern – the collapse of any semblance of unity, solidarity or common understanding among the Arabs.

The Arab world was once again in complete disarray. The common denominators that brought the so-called revolution- ary or reactionary states together had disappeared. Syria was quarrelling with Egypt and Iraq, Saudi Arabia and Egypt were feuding over the Yemen, Algeria was fighting with Morocco and Morocco was irritated by Tunisia's recognition of Mauritania. In the midst of this confusion and misunder- standing, an alarming new turn of events in Palestine brought the Arabs briefly to their senses and awakened them to the real danger threatening the security of the states and the stability of their politics. The new factors on this occasion were Israel's plan to divert the headwaters of the Jordan river and the emergence of the Palestine guerrilla movement. As clashes increased in frequency and ferocity on both the Jordanian and the Syrian fronts, the Arabs became concerned about the outbreak of another war – a war which they did not seek and realized they could not win in their divided state.

The emergence of the guerrilla movement was the direct result of the continuous and relentless radicalization of the Arab political process. Furthermore, the guerrillas had an invested interest in the further identification of rampant radicalism that ensured its own survival. Some fifteen years after the dispersal of the Palestine Arabs, the majority of whom had become destitute refugees upon the establishment of the state of Israel in their ancestral homeland, many of them had come to the conclusion that their national cause had been ill served by the Arab states acting on their behalf and in their defence. Several groups of young Palestinians, mostly students and graduates of Arab as well as foreign universities, had come together to advocate a new departure in the struggle for the restoration of Palestine. In a decade that had heard so much of "peoples' wars" and "wars of national liberation", these groups sought to seize the initiative in their national struggle. They wanted to establish their right to speak for their own people and decide their destiny. They asserted their own national identity as Palestinians as well as Arabs, a consciousness different and separate from traditional Pan-Arabism, an affiliation identified with a specific territory: that of Palestine. The consequence of this assertion was a summons to Palestinians to take up arms and engage the enemy, namely the state of Israel.

It was only natural for the Palestine Arabs, frustrated by their long exile and oppression, that they should come to such a conclusion. However, they were almost unaware of the serious implications that their actions would entail. What they did not take into consideration, or indeed comprehend, was that they could not act as free and independent individuals. Essentially, they were Palestinians; but in all the Arab states except Jordan (where they were granted the full rights of citizenship) they were refugees, for whom their hosts, however sympathetic they might feel towards the Palestine Arabs' cause, could not jeopardize their own national interest or abandon their international obligations.

It was clear to all the Arab states that the new strategy advocated by the new generation of Palestine Arabs amounted to an invitation to war with Israel; a war which the Arab states were not prepared to wage through lack of military preparations and the absence of a joint Arab strategy. Faced with this dangerous prospect and with Israeli retaliation to guerrilla activity increasing, Egypt, which had ended its self-imposed isolation with its intervention in the Yemen in 1962, called for an Arab summit conference of heads of state to deliberate on the grave situation towards the end of 1963. Summitry has become a permanent feature of Arab politics and practically a substitute for the regular sessions of the Arab League.

The early summit meetings were marked by vagueness of purpose and lack of preparation, both on the issue of the Jordan water rights and on the guerrillas. The only tangible outcome was the creation of the Palestine Liberation Organization in 1964. The politics of the PLO and its relations with the Arab states further distracted attention from the Arab political process and diverted essential energies that could have contributed to its evolution. The designation of the PLO as the sole legitimate representative of the Palestine people by the Rabat Arab summit conference in 1974 led Jordan, for instance, to suspend its parliamentary life. After a period of several years during which the National Consultative Council substituted for the Jordanian parliament, Jordan has now decided to restore its constitutional parliamentary government so that all its citizens will have a say in the decision-making process.

However, summitry – there have been twelve such meetings in the last twenty years – has not ameliorated the plight of the Palestinians, contained their national movement, satisfied their political aspirations or (still more significantly) prevented wars with Israel. With two more wars in 1967 and 1973, the prolonged and even more damaging war in the Gulf between two Muslim countries, and the brutal and tragic destruction of Lebanon, the Arab East is confronted with graver dangers and a more ominous and uncertain future. War abroad and internal fragmentation threaten the region. War, instability, radicalization – these features have consumed the energies of the Arab people. They have not been able to devote much time to the development of the political process.

Today, the politics of the middle ground, steering a deliberate middle course, which has been Jordan's response to the politics of the extremes, faces serious dangers that threaten not only to undermine the political process of all states in the region, but to jeopardize their very survival. Irredentist, populist and religiously fanatical political movements all over the Middle East have had an abrupt impact on Arab society and politics. The denial of legitimate rights, compounded by the absence of authoritative public institutions to safeguard the pluralist composition of Arab society and to maintain its ethnic and religious diversity, has allowed rampant extremism to dominate the conduct of public affairs. Social diversity has assumed an ever-increasing importance in the struggle for power and dominance among popularistic organizations of different origins and divergent aims. The politics of fanaticism have added a new dimension to social conflict and the polarization of communities. Primordial perceptions of society, of an increasingly exclusive tendency, have absorbed the ideology of these extremist groups. The continuation of this trend will not only further undermine the development of a sound, healthy and representative political process, but it will contribute to the fragmentation of all the states of the region, as it has done to the most successive pluralist state, the Lebanon, in the last few years.

3 The Political Economy

No assessment of the current problems of the Arab East would be complete without consideration of its economic factors. These factors all too commonly dominate such consideration by the rest of the world. While the present configuration of territory and people is determined as well by the historical and political dimensions, the economic dimension completes the picture. This is a novel factor. While long-range economic considerations have long been part of Western European international relations, their impact on the Arab scene has released forces that are still not fully realized.

Our objective is to indicate the parameters of the general direction of economic events and trends, and how they relate to the basic needs and requirements of the Arab people, and to attempt an examination of the factors that influence the emergence of a new economic order in the region. Change, especially in the economic field, has been rapid, even breathless. It has already led many contemporary Arab intellectuals to the conclusion that, by economic pressure alone, the Arabs have not only transformed their societies but precipitated the evolution of a new and modern Arab. He is educated, work-oriented, mobile; a discerning, sophisticated, even cosmopolitan person. This new Arab exists, but his novelty should not blind us to the presence of the other type, traditional in outlook, religiously conservative, resistant to change and opposed to present prosperity as an indication of modern decadence.

It is the conflict between those two stereotype figures that the Arab East has now to accommodate, on terms acceptable to both. Without such an accommodation, the social and political dislocations that have accompanied social change threaten the very foundations of Arab society. Violence and revolution may soon be the only means of development. Arabs have seen too much turmoil. It has invariably been detrimental to the evolution of a new and authentic Arab culture, the legitimate heir to the past glories that Arabs have contributed to world civilization.

The main focus of this chapter is the economic performance of Jordan. An attempt will be made to identify the pattern of development, as well as of economic management, which may yet affect the region as a whole. I shall consider the present economic realities against the background of the nature and direction of recent patterns of development. By doing so, it becomes possible to identify alternative approaches to the management of economic affairs.

Economic studies and publications, both scholarly and official, abound. Numerous development plans for various countries in the region have been drawn up, assessed and analysed by different specialists, as well as by regional and international organizations. There is a long list of official and semi-official publications extolling the merits of one particular economic plan rather than others. What I want to do is to journey along the path where politics and economics mix, interchange and interact. It is admittedly a grey area, but such a combination is characteristic of Arab economic development as of the Third World in general. It helps to examine and explain the nature of the relationship between the two fields so far as development plans are concerned and to assess the role that certain political or ideological considerations play in the formulation of economic policy.

It is vital to obtain a better understanding of the interplay between politics and economics in the making of development plans. If the Arab East is to survive, reorientation will be required in so far as economic planning is concerned. For too long Arab states have planned their policies in accordance with some alien and untested ideological formulation which is not directly related to the needs and requirements of the Arabs today and exists only in a vacuum. In order to have a proper appreciation of the economic dimension and the peoples' aspirations for the future, a complete overhaul of contemporary policies may not be amiss.

Historical parallels

Certain basic natural characteristics have influenced the economic life of the Arab East continuously since ancient times. The story of the early periods of economic progress and prosperity of the great civilizations within the two major river basins (the Nile valley to the west and the Tigris-Euphrates to the east) bounding the largely arid or semi-arid Arab East is well known. Numerous periods of prosperity occurred in other parts of the region throughout its long history. The two common features of all these cycles of growth were the harnessing of water resources and the exploitation of the geographical position of the region as a gateway in international trade between Europe and the Eastern Mediterranean on the one hand and the Far East and Africa on the other. The provision of security through strong centralized governments was a common factor in all these cycles of progress. A powerful central authority was essential for the safeguarding and maintenance of the extensive and vulnerable irrigation systems, for the exploitation of minerals and for the protection of the caravan traffic of ancient trade routes.

The impact of geography on the political economy of the region is especially apparent in the area that comprises modern Jordan, lying as it does between the fertile crescent and the arid desert, where the age-old struggle between "the desert and the sown" continues to the present day.

The harnessing of water resources in the Arab East was achieved through extensive and intricate water conservation and irrigation systems. Remarkable skill was devoted to these enterprises and the frontier of the desert was steadily pushed back. In Nabatean times progress was made in the area of present-day Jordan, both in conserving every source of water for agricultural use and in exploiting the mineral wealth of the area. In at least one period of ancient growth, development based upon the mineral wealth of Wadi Araba, south of the

73

Dead Sea, became extensive enough to shift the centre of activity from north to south, where copper was smelted and exported through Aqaba to the east in return for spice and gold.

The long history of the Arab East shows numerous cycles of decay and growth. The last cycle saw the onset of slow decline between the twelfth and eighteenth centuries, followed by a period of gradual revival from the nineteenth century onwards, when the frontiers of cultivation and settlement were substantially extended within the area of the fertile crescent. The introduction of central government for the first time in centuries and a rise in the demand for agricultural products are the two most important factors behind this cycle of revival during the nineteenth century and down to the First World War.

Greater stability and economic growth came as a result of the Egyptian occupation of Syria in the 1830s and of a more effective Ottoman central administration in the latter part of the century. Many areas that had lain waste for centuries were resettled and cultivated as a result of their pacification. The increased demand for agricultural products was generated by trends both within the region and outside it.

Within the region, the decline of the death rate that occurred through improved health conditions resulted in a population growth that placed increased pressure on available food supplies. From a level of about 1.3 million in the 1890s, the population of Greater Syria (Syria, Lebanon, Jordan and Palestine) is estimated to have nearly trebled by 1910, when it reached a level of about 3.5 million. A further stimulus to agricultural expansion came from outside the region as a result of the rise in the demand for agricultural products that occurred in Europe from the middle of the nineteenth century onwards.

Besides its direct influence on agriculture and population, the introduction of centralized modern administrations within the political boundaries created in the region following the First World War settlement gave an added impetus to economic expansion in other respects. For example, cadastral surveys were undertaken during the inter-war period in a number of countries, among them Iraq, Syria and Jordan, which provided the basis for reorganizing land tenure, hitherto undetermined or based on ill-defined traditional rights. Increased military expenditure within the region, and the restrictions on imports that occurred during the Second World War, gave a further spur to economic growth.

Jordan, the *carrefour des nations*, is a land of physical contrasts. The Jordan valley itself is the most remarkable example, its whole length, as it runs south, like "a green serpent" between the pale mountains of the east and the faint mosaic of the western land. Its thick vegetation is uncompromisingly distinct throughout its entire course, its colour living green with, here and there, a flash of broken water or a subdued patch of brown interrupting the verdure.

Historically, Jordan attained most of its importance because it was part of a wider area; it was the hinge, so to speak, that linked the sharply contrasted zones that lay to north and south, east and west. The political developments that began with the advent of the twentieth century once again placed Jordan at the centre of events, and brought into high relief its potential regional role as a "middle ground", in more senses than one, in the Arab East.

Politics and the political economy: a new way to past glories

The process of modern political events in the Arab East which was examined in the previous chapter is vividly reflected in the economic life of the region. Manifestations of this political process are clearly visible not only in the economic aspirations and expectations expressed by individuals and groups, but also in the field of national economic policy. Evidently, wealth and economic progress and individual well-being are an essential part of the past glories that the Arabs have now been attempting to recapture and recreate. From some points of view the whole process of political events in the Arab East in the modern era is vividly reflected in the course of economic events and the economic life of the region. The echoes, if not the tremors, of this political process, underway from the nineteenth century down to the present day, can be heard and felt clearly over the whole range of economic policies, trends and changes that our* area has witnessed throughout these years. In the post Second World War period, and especially since the oil boom of 1973, the quickening pace of events and the more complex interaction, even entanglement, of politics and economics had by the early 1980s precipitated a situation full of promise – whether for disaster or for progress and stability during the last decades of the twentieth century remains to be seen. Which it will be is beyond prediction – or rather prophecy. I will try rather to identify some of the chances for success and failure in the game of economic snakes and ladders in which all Arabs are involved. A balanced view should neither minimize nor condemn economic achieve-ments, nor evade the political and socio-economic issues that must be squarely faced and adequately tackled. There are plenty of lessons to be learned from recent trends and events.

With the advent of the twentieth century there was an acceleration in the political process that had developed during the previous hundred years. A longing for the past glories of the Arabs and Islam gathered momentum; with it went an increased call for their reconstruction. The modes of thinking and the rationale behind the political doctrines thus arti-culated were vividly reflected in a rapidly developing conven-tional wisdom in the economic field. The issues of freedom from foreign rule and Arab independence all had their place in a new golden image of the future. As the twentieth century progressed, it came to be increasingly believed that independence would immediately result in prosperity through the exploitation and development of economic resources for the benefit of the indigenous population instead of the foreign imperialists. Arab unity, by simple extension of the political conventional wisdom into the economic field, would be swiftly and automatically followed by the emergence and development of a modern, industrialized Arab economy rivalling that of any modern industrialized Western power.

Trends in economic policy

The course of political events from the introduction of the liberal system of government to its failure and the ensuing radicalization of politics had a clearly visible economic dimension. To put it simply, it is only natural that the political policies advocated to meet political aspirations or adopted to achieve political objectives should be extended into the economic field. Whereas between the two World Wars the economic bent of political action was based on private enterprise, the radicalization of politics in the late 1950s and early 1960s was natural alongside the adoption of radical economic policies such as the "socialist" economic measures implemented in Egypt under Nasser. During the union with Syria, similar nationalization and agrarian reform measures were introduced in Syria, which had hitherto developed as a private-enterprise and mercantile community on traditional lines.

The break-up of the United Arab Republic through the withdrawal of Syria in 1961 was swiftly followed by the abrogation of these socialist measures, which were, however, reimposed when the Baath socialists took over power soon after. Such a pattern occurred in a number of other instances. Eventually the radicalization of politics induced a transformation in economic policy. Many of the Arab states adopted the socialist approach simply as a vehicle to strengthen and accelerate their reformist political programmes. Some countries, and their leaders, have been more radical than others. In all, once national liberation has been achieved, the establishment of a fairer and less corrupt society requires a visible change in economic relationships. The objective is a self-sufficient economy free from foreign exploitation and domination.

Socialist policies and practices have always been asserted to be identical with such measures as would ensure economic liberation and independence. There is, therefore, no easy definition of the doctrine known as Arab socialism distinct from these goals. There are no separate foundations, rooted in Arab society or thought, for such a creed. It can only be defined in terms of government measures undertaken to ensure a fairer distribution of national wealth. It is difficult, therefore, to distinguish Arab socialism except as an instrument of national policy. The absence of any uniform theoretical framework from which socialist thought and practices are derived is clear evidence that different countries determine their own approach to socialist objectives.

Islam and socialist economy

Rapid economic development accompanied by large-scale movements of population from the rural areas into the cities and towns, with its concomitant problems of urbanization, gave deep concern to religious authorities worried about the moral well-being of the community. This concern was soon transformed into an active political movement commonly known as Islamic resurgence or Muslim fundamentalism. The movement as such is not new. In many ways it is as old as Islam itself. What is new and wearisome about it is that it has acquired both the political activism and the vocabulary generally associated with the different variants of Marxist ideology.

In common with the radical nationalists, the Muslim fundamentalists' consciousness and concern about social iniquities, moral deprivation and economic exploitation obliged them to veer towards the promotion of a kind of socialist doctrine, akin to an Islamic version of collectivism. Its more extreme types have been described as Islamic Marxism. Though the majority of Muslim fundamentalists abhor Marxist notions of historical determinism, the inevitability of the class struggle and dialectical materialism, they share with the extremist wings of the movement their denunciation of imperialism and capitalism, the twin evils to which the motives and means of Western domination are ascribed. Their apprehensions have led to the formulation of an Islamic socialist programme whose implementation would relieve the poverty and misery of the masses.

However, like their radical nationalist counterparts, the fundamentalists could not escape the implied contradictions

78

in their socialist beliefs thus formulated. There was a danger that their creed might concentrate on a Muslim egalitarianism, which could in the long run lead to greater domination by the state and its socialist proponents. The institution of private property, for example, has posed a particular difficulty. All strands of Muslim fundamentalism feel bound to honour it as a cardinal right, but its effects are seen as the root cause of social evils, and therefore to be changed by political action. Without denying its significance, they have attempted to tamper with its application. Private ownership has a social function. It is accompanied by a public utility: a kind of social security provided by the rich for the poor. Normally, charity is essentially a voluntary activity, but, if it is lacking, the state must intervene to fill the gap. It is derived from the precept that Muslims, all members of the community, are entitled to share all the goods which the community provides. Yet there is no justification, in the conflict between materialism and religion, for making religion the vehicle for new concepts whose real roots lie in materialism, which reflects novel beliefs alien to religion.

The majority of fundamentalists reject the concept of class conflict and the proletarian revolution in favour of the social harmony and co-operation between the various elements that make up society. Public ownership of the means of production and nationalization are allowed on the grounds that the higher and more important requirements of the community take precedence over those of the individual. The ultimate justification for public ownership is that all property stems from the sovereignty of God, to whom all the resources of the earth belong: man enjoys these gifts on trust to use and develop them by honest toil for his own good and for that of the community at large.

The interaction between Muslims and advocates of Marxist beliefs and methodology has produced an ambiguity similar to that which characterized the early exchanges between Islam and the West. All Muslims, modernists or fundamentalists, see no possible reconciliation, no compatibility between Islam and atheistic communist materialism. They insist that their religion must be viewed as separate and different from any ideology derived from alien historical and philosophical sources.

Under these restrictions, it is fairly obvious that no synthesis is possible between Islamic tenets and Marxist ideology. If Islam may share common objectives with European ideologies, this is no warrant to identify one with the others; still less should one conclude that they are based on the same principles. Nonetheless, there are trends in Islam today which have been proved to be as revolutionary as the Marxist tenets that their advocates despise and condemn. They have substituted a millenarian Islamic rehabilitation of the universe for Marxist determinism. The purpose is to make Islam the sole basis of ideology, with the notion of the Way of God (*sunnat Allah*) as equivalent to the laws of evolution. They claim that God's evolutionary processes will lead to the completion of the struggle between good and evil, terminating in the establishment of a righteous society in which the toilers of the earth will triumph. Those tendencies point to an overwhelming need for the evolution of a universal and open concept of analogy (*qiyǎs*) to the thought and experience of others within the Islamic world.

All these revolutionary trends appear, in fact, to be solely motivated by economic need. In their restrictive provisions for material benefits, they cast off a fundamental element, a cardinal feature, of Muslim civilization: namely, tolerance. Genuine belief in Islam demands absolute submission to the will of God and an irrevocable admission of His lordship and majesty. The commitment to Islam requires the liberation and purification of the soul so that moral and spiritual salvation, contentment and supremacy may be secured. Pursuit of materialism and class wars, by whatever name they are called, will not achieve that.

The political economy of legitimacy

We discussed previously how the great expectations unleashed by the political process in the decades after the First World War were invariably unrealized and how failure and frustration ensued. Paradoxically, the elusiveness of the glorious past and the resultant failure to make any visible progress in the political field made economic progress more difficult to achieve, yet, at the same time, all the more vehemently advocated and espoused by politicians and ideologues. Lack of progress in the political arena stimulated the resort to economic development as a double panacea, "substituting for", or "complementing", political action (or rather failure). On the one hand, if the glories of the past could not be recreated and reconstructed in the political sense, then economic glories would perhaps be a compensatory substitute. On the other hand, as political failure brings the legitimacy of rulers and regimes into question, there is an increasing tendency to legitimate political power through the means of economic development. Support for political power or a regime in danger of failure could thus be achieved by a rapid process of economic development, creating visible achievements (industries, ports, major schemes and works) with little or no consideration given to the ability of the socio-political system to absorb or maintain such achievements successfully.

The advent of oil

Such patterns and trends in economic policy crystallized and gathered momentum immediately after the Second World War. The entanglement of the political process with the conflict in Palestine rendered it much more complex; the strife thus generated brought about the first Arab–Israeli conflict in 1948, and that precipitated further upheavals in the 1950s. By that time the economies of the different states in the region had attained increased, but varied, levels of development and expansion through the process of general economic revival previously mentioned. In Egypt, Syria, Lebanon and Palestine modern manufacturing industries in textiles, food production and construction materials flourished. Projects for water development in both Egypt and Iraq (the areas of the region's two great ancient river-basin civilizations) were initiated. It is not my purpose here to analyse or quantify the economic developments and trends that occurred during that period. Suffice it to say that by the mid-century both the psychological climate and the progress achieved in the first half of the century had helped to lay the ground and prepare the region for a period of further economic construction and growth. The ensuing decades, from the 1950s to the present day, however, saw, apart from what might be termed the further "politicizing" of economic policies, the unforeseen and unprecedented expansion of the financial resources available within the region through the oil boom. The advent of the oil boom in the Arab East added further impetus to factors already at work and moved the Arab community still more rapidly along the path on which it had embarked at the turn of the century.

Oil and the "super-development plan"

Oil revenues in the region were already on an upward trend during the 1950s and 1960s but leaped to unprecedented levels in the wake of the 1973 Arab–Israeli war. This posed a dual challenge: in the first place, oil revenues provided readily available financial resources to governments, which encouraged them to ambitious development plans; in the second place, they also presented an extra challenge to the authorities to do more for the benefit of "the people", and thereby to reconstruct the "glorious past" more quickly, if not at once, now that funds and finance were no longer in short supply. Many states came closer and closer to a position in which unlimited supplies of capital were available for development, without (at least in some instances) the labour resources to benefit from it. About two decades before the 1973 oil boom, Nuri al-Said in Iraq diverted a fixed proportion of oil revenues directly to the budget of the Development Board to be used for economic development. What thus began as a perfectly logical and natural method for utilizing oil wealth to accelerate development was extended rapidly as oil revenues grew, regardless of the absorptive capacity of the different economies or of the impact of such investments on the social and human fabric. Perhaps it was difficult or even impossible to avoid such a course of events: the temptations and pressures confronting the decision-maker and planner were too difficult to resist.

This process culminated in the late 1970s in the phenomenon of the "super-development plan", a concept given its fullest extension in Iran. "Super-saturating the economy" with "hyper-investment", regardless of its impact on society and the individual, became the name of the game. The involvement of governments in the economy increased to the point where it became difficult, if not impossible, to distinguish between oil revenues, the government budget and national income (or between the government and the economy, for that matter). And this was not only the case in socialist-oriented states, but also in so-called conservative states with a private enterprise system. A new species of "capitalist" central planning swiftly emerged.

It is relevant to note that political collapse occurred in Iran despite the super-development plans and extensive invest-ment programmes under the Shah. How far such economic policies accelerated (or retarded, for that matter) the collapse of the Shah's rule in Iran it is not my purpose to evaluate. But the collapse took place notwithstanding the economic policies adopted by the Shah. In other words, stability and progress require, at the least, other components than super-develop-ment plans, despite their promise of a short-cut to material plenty and paradise on earth, all within one or two genera-tions. Attempts at distributing wealth and spreading plenty are no substitute for addressing the political realities of participation and power-sharing. To be sure, the capitalistic approach to the planning of oil economics, "neo-central" in the sense that it tries to restrain free enterprise by reference to the common good, has as much chance of success as that of "socialist" central planning. As we shall see, the moderate approach of centrism, an economic policy of the middle ground, offers perhaps a more promising and viable alternative.

As we have seen, frustrations and lack of visible progress in the political field stimulated the adoption of economic development as a political tool. In its extreme form, the super-development plan that emerged in the 1970s, the initial stimulus, both towards substituting economic policies for political ones as a means of recapturing past glories, and towards utilizing economic development to support a regime, can be clearly identified. Needless to say, the emergence of the super-development plan, with its hardware shopping lists in billions of dollars, found a very receptive and encouraging audience amongst the stagflation-weary industrialists of the West.

Society and the individual

This sudden and extensive change in economic conditions had a far-reaching impact on society and the individual. The oil boom affected both the community and the individual, not only through the impact of government budgets, but also through the new attitudes that it stimulated in the private sector. What might be termed a "gold-rush" mentality increasingly dominated the policies and commercial activities of investors and entrepreneurs. Speculative investments became increasingly predominant in the private sector and in certain instances investments in industries and enterprises would be undertaken without proper evaluation or adequate management. A quantitative expansion without a qualitative change occurred and certain private industries – construction, for instance – even suffered a decline in the level of efficiency under the impact of rapid expansion in scale.

These side effects associated with the oil boom were not restricted to the oil countries themselves. Through official government-to-government transfers, in the form of loans and other economic support, and through the migration of manpower and the consequent workers' remittances, the symptoms were transmitted in varying degrees across the national boundaries of all the states, oil-producing or not, of the Arab East. This partly accounts for the inflation and real estate booms experienced in the so-called socialist economies, where prices and property values soared at rates that rivalled or exceeded those in the most private of the private-sector economies.

If economic development was resorted to as a substitute for, and complement to, political action (or lack of it) in the Arab East, the results have had an hysterical intensity. Inflation, rapid uncontrolled urbanization, social tensions resulting from swift economic change and widening differences in income levels, and all the other dislocating impacts of ever-larger investment programmes, far from diffusing or reducing the initial political tensions and frustrations in the different societies of the Arab East, will in reality augment such tensions, increase polarization and alienation between society and government on the one hand and, on the other, within society itself, between the haves and the have nots.

To sum up at this point, all the foregoing patterns and trends are in reality only a mirror image in economic terms of the political process. The frustrations experienced by succeeding generations of Arabs have, as it were, become part of their thought processes and have thus caused the attempts at reconstruction without proper foundations. Such a perspective will clarify and explain the nature of otherwise incomprehensible-seeming phenomena, such as the super-development plan, hyper-investment, entrepreneurial behavioural patterns, and the real-estate and stock-exchange booms and crashes, the most notorious of which has been the episode of the Al Manakh market in Kuwait, involving reported losses of 25 billion dollars in 1982.

It may be useful at this stage to add that, historically, central planning has been associated with the emergence of radical socialist economies. Apart from the so-called socialist countries in the Arab East, we have seen that a new type of central planning in the private-enterprise oil economies emerged. The scope and extent of capitalist central planning reached such extremes that the differentiation between government and the economy became increasingly difficult to discern. Beyond the role of central planning usually existing in radical or collectivist political systems, the government assumed the role of benefactor, subsidizer and (in the last resort) bailer-out for the private sector when it got into difficulties due to reckless attempts at speculative investments and mal-utilization of transplanted modern economic organizations, such as stock exchanges and commercial banks.

Just as certain institutions that were transplanted into the political sphere – such as parliaments – did not function as initially expected, so in the economic field the transplantation of institutions and ideas had similar results. For example, while the real purpose of a stock exchange is to mobilize capital for industrial investments, stock exchanges became increasingly utilized for speculative investments of excess funds without creating productive enterprises to balance them. I am not arguing against the introduction of modern institutions or techniques, but it is clear that such machinery has to be introduced and allowed to evolve in a manner compatible with the social and cultural realities within the different states. Success depends on our ability to build economic and political institutions, policies and systems with due consideration for the structure and norms of the community that the planners and decision-makers are trying to develop. For any programme of action to succeed, it must be based on a proper knowledge and understanding of the past and present realities of our societies and the nature of trends recently at work.

The Jordanian achievement: economic trends since 1948

As we have seen, historically, more importance has been attached to Jordan through its geographical position and its strategic role as a bridge between other communities than for any natural endowment of resources or wealth within its boundaries. It is hardly surprising then that our successive economic development plans in Jordan since the early 1950s have had two salient features: the development of our water resources for agricultural use and the construction of the basic transportation and other facilities providing links through Jordan for the region as a whole. While historical parallels can be drawn easily here, two features of our achievements in modern times that are without previous parallel have been the success with which we have shouldered the burden of a sudden influx of population and the development of our region as a whole through the provision of skilled manpower resources.

The story of our remarkable socio-economic development and progress since the tragic events in Palestine in 1948 has been documented in statistical and economic surveys, such as our successive economic development plans. During this period, Jordan has achieved one of the highest rates of economic growth to be found amongst the developing countries. Throughout the period from the mid-1950s to the present day, the Gross Domestic Product increased at an average annual rate of about 8 per cent in real terms, except for a brief interruption in the aftermath of the Middle East war in 1967 when the West Bank fell under Israeli occupation.

During those years, hundreds of thousands of Palestinians lost their homes and means of livelihood twice within one generation, in 1948 and again in 1967. The full force of the demographic upheaval caused by this human and political tragedy fell on Jordan, but, despite the heavy refugee burden which we had to shoulder, and despite the rapid natural rate of increase of our population, which has recently exceeded 3 per cent per annum, the even more rapid rate of growth of GNP has resulted in the attainment of a rise in real *per capita* income of about 5 per cent annually over the last three decades. By 1982, *per capita* income on the East Bank reached a level of 2000 dollars, which brings us to an intermediate level among the developing countries. Although a lot remains to be done, this has helped to provide a better life for Jordanians; we have secured basic human needs for the majority of our population affected by the upheavals of 1948 and 1967.

Throughout the 1950s and 1960s, our rapid rate of economic growth was achieved within the framework of a remarkable monetary stability, with the rate of inflation averaging about 2 per cent annually. However, by the 1970s, the rate of inflation climbed, initially to 5 per cent (1967–1972) and eventually to about 12 per cent annually (1973–1981). More recently, we have managed to bring down our rate of inflation to single figures (7 per cent during 1982) and we are still trying to reduce inflationary pressures. To be sure, the substantial expansion of our investment programme during the 1970s (when capital formation reached a level of about 50 per cent of GDP), coupled with the impact of world inflationary trends, forced us to sustain nearly a decade of two-figure inflation, a phenomenon previously unknown to Jordan. It has left its damaging impact on our social fabric, and we will continue to give top priority to anti-inflationary measures, which we have seen to yield adjustments in the desired direction.

We have substantial and practical results to show. Whether in the development of our water and agricultural resources in the Jordan valley and the highlands, or in the exploitation of such mineral wealth as we possess, on the eastern plateau (phosphates) and in the Rift Valley (potash from the Dead Sea), it is clear that a rapid and solid structural transformation has been achieved during this period. (Mineral development in southern Jordan brings to mind the ancient periods of growth in the southern Rift Valley mentioned earlier.) It is true that, in view of our heavy population and defence burdens, we have had to rely substantially on external resources. But the fact that the rate of gross domestic capital formation from the mid-1970s to the early 1980s has been around 40–50 per cent of our GDP, compared with 15 and 20 per cent during the 1950s and 1960s, shows that we have made good use of any external support that has been made available. In fact, this rate of capital formation is one of the highest achieved by any of the developing countries and indicates the extent of the absorptive capacity of our economy. Within the span of three decades we have managed to "sink" a significant and increasing proportion of the total resources at our disposal in such a way as to create within this relatively short period a solid foundation of socio-economic infrastructure. The rapid embodiment of these resources into our economic structure has not only managed to meet the infrastructural and productive gaps and dislocations generated by successive Arab–Israeli conflicts, but has additionally provided a platform for future progress, both for Jordan and its region.

The rapid growth of investment, employment and output in our primary and secondary sectors (agriculture, mining, manufacturing, power-generation, construction and transportation) has been paralleled by a rapid growth in GDP originating in the tertiary sectors of the economy (comprising retail trade, banking, government services and other services, including education). Certainly, over the last thirty years the tertiary sectors of our economy – that is, broadly defined, the "services sector" – have had a relatively high share (50–60 per cent) in our economy, both in terms of employment and production. This factor (there are a number of reasons for it, such as our heavy reliance on external resources and the heavy refugee burden) has been a cause of worry to our planners, who have advocated the development of a more structurally balanced economy, emphasising the development of the commodity-producing primary and secondary sectors.

Commodity exports, not only from our agricultural and mineral sectors, but more recently from manufacturing industry, have been rising at a rapid rate and reached (together with re-exports) a level of over three-quarters of a billion dollars by 1982, compared with less than 5 million dollars in the early fifties and only about 30 million dollars in the mid-1960s. But despite this speedy growth, our balance of trade has remained in chronic deficit, due to the large import bill imposed on us by the two burdens of population growth and defence. Our commodity imports increased from about 30 million dollars in the early 1950s to around 108 million dollars by the mid-1960s and exceeded 3 billion dollars by 1982. Accordingly, by 1982, our trade gap had reached a level exceeding 2.5 billion dollars. In addition to the official aid received by the country from oil-producing Arab states supporting our moderate and constructive regional role, our net earnings from invisibles (including remittances from Jordanians working abroad) have increasingly helped to balance our trade deficit. Unlike many non-oil-producing countries, we have resorted to external borrowing only to a limited extent, and that primarily to finance productive investments. Our total external public debt stood recently at

1.7 billion dollars, compared with our gold and foreign exchange reserves of about 2 billion dollars.

It is worth noting at this juncture that the rapid growth of our imports has been accompanied by a basic transformation in their structure. Whereas throughout the 1950s and 1960s about two thirds of our import bill consisted of consumer goods, by the late 1970s and early 1980s the proportion was reversed, with consumer goods falling to about one-third, the remaining two-thirds of our imports being comprised of raw materials and capital goods. Thus, of our 3 billion dollar import bill in 1982, about 2.2 billion dollars consisted of raw materials and capital goods.

At the official level, and throughout this period, Jordan did all it could to promote economic co-operation amongst Arab states. Official efforts for furthering economic co-operation take place within the framework of the Arab League, through the Arab Economic Council and specialized economic organizations, as well as the Arab Economic Unity Council. In 1964 this Council established the Arab Common Market, of which Jordan was a founding member. The resolutions and agreements concluded within this official framework have been implemented amongst the different states to limited and varying extents, depending on general political conditions; a great deal remains to be done in this direction.

More recently, the Arab summit held at Amman in 1980 endorsed a document for the strategy of joint Arab economic action until the year 2000, which set three goals: Arab unity, development and integration. The 1980s were pronounced to be a "development decade" and an initial joint Arab development fund of 5 billion dollars was established towards assisting in financing projects in the less developed Arab countries. The implementation of these plans has, however, remained problematic.

The demographic dimension

While historical parallels between ancient and new can be drawn in the Arab East in the field of the development of water resources and trade routes, Jordan's modern demographic role in the region has had no parallel either within the context of the Arab–Israeli conflict or of the oil boom in neighbouring countries. The exploitation of Jordan's water, mineral and trade resources in the modern era has, by contrast, been paralleled in ancient times. But our investment in recent years in human resources, and the role that these human resources have played within the Arab East, are a completely new factor.

The population of both the East and West Banks stood at less than 1 million people on the eve of the first Arab–Israeli war in 1946 (the World Bank gives a figure of 855,000 for both). This settled population was augmented by 42 per cent during 1948 through the inflow of about 350,000 Palestinian refugees to both Banks. The 1961 census gave a total population figure of about 1.7 million, divided almost equally between the West Bank (800,000) and East Bank (900,000). Today, nearly a quarter of a century after the 1961 census, the population of the West Bank (together with that of East Jerusalem Arabs) still stands at roughly the same level, while that of the East Bank has nearly trebled to over 2.5 million. Thus, in addition to the demographic upheaval of 1948, the occupation of the West Bank by Israel since 1967 has resulted in the effective depopulation and stagnation of the West Bank, while the burden of a further influx of population has been imposed on the East Bank. By 1983, out of the total of nearly 2 million Palestinian refugees registered with UNRWA, about 56 per cent were registered in the East and West Banks (759,000 and 344,000 respectively), while the remaining 850,000 were registered in Lebanon, Syria and the Gaza strip.

It is important to note that the population dislocations since 1948 were accompanied by no less severe economic disruptions. First, both the East and West Banks had to cope after 1948 with the severance of their direct trade and communications routes with the Mediterranean via the coastal plains, which became part of Israel. Throughout the 1950s and 1960s, Jordan had to invest heavily to create a substitute economic infrastructure. Second, a further disruption occurred after the severance of normal links between both

Banks in 1967, when Israel occupied the West Bank and imposed selective and undirectional controls of trade and other economic links between both Banks.

Jordan has suffered most, among the different states of the Arab East, from the demographic aspect of the Arab–Israeli conflict. From the outset, however, it has taken the most active steps to shoulder the burden of these responsibilities in the region. Our investments in education, manpower development and social services since 1948 have done more than help to alleviate the consequences of the major human tragedy that afflicted the Arabs of Palestine; but the economic growth of the area as a whole has benefited by providing the skilled manpower resources badly needed by the oil countries, where about 400,000 Jordanian nationals are employed today, together with their dependents. In fact, about as many Jordanians are economically active on the East Bank as outside the country in the neighbouring oil states. (The labour force on the East Bank was estimated at 450,000 in 1981.) Although remittances from our labour force abroad (about 1 billion dollars through the banking system in 1982) have helped towards meeting our chronic foreign trade deficit, the costs to the country have been substantial in terms of the drain on the best of our skilled manpower resources.

This manpower and brain drain is a phenomenon faced by many developing countries all over the world, as well as within our region – in Lebanon, Syria, Egypt. Despite the valuable contribution of remittances from those working abroad to the foreign-exchange earnings of the manpower exporting countries, the national economy of these countries loses the substantial indirect return from its investment in manpower. With this view, and in order to maintain labour movement as a mutually beneficial activity, both to the labour-exporting and host countries, in 1977 I proposed the establishment of an International Labour Compensatory Facility (ILCF). The proposed facility will be allocated to developing labour-exporting countries in proportions relative to the cost incurred by the loss of labour. This proposal is still under consideration by the relevant United Nations agencies.

Today, about 877,000 Jordanians are students in schools and in higher education. This represents 35 per cent of our population of 2.5 million. Out of this number, about 82,000 are enrolled in higher education both in Jordan and abroad. Our commitment to education, to research and development and to science and technology is shown by the development of three universities in Jordan, as well as the Royal Scientific Society, our centre for scientific research and the transfer of higher technology.

Women have traditionally been viewed as playing a secondary role in the life of the countries of the Arab East. Our socio-economic transformation in Jordan has been accompanied by the increasing participation of women in all aspects of our life. In terms of education, the total number of Jordanians at schools (796,000) is closely divided between males (425,000) and females (371,000). Although, due to our high rate of population growth and the age structure of our population, our total participation rates (the ratio of the labour force to the total population) are on the low side (20 per cent), the ratio of females within the labour force has been rising – from 10 per cent in the mid-1970s to about 18 per cent recently.

The 1979 census indicated that about 51 per cent of our population on the East Bank were fourteen years of age or less. This young age structure of our population, together with the low level of participation by women in the labour force, in fact accounts for the low labour-force ratio in our total population, which imposes further burdens on our social infra-structural facilities. Thus, while only one-fifth of our population are wage earners, in more advanced countries with a more balanced age structure this ratio reaches a level of over one-third.

A centrist economic policy

Thus, despite heavy burdens and limited resources, Jordan has managed to achieve remarkable socio-economic progress. While placing emphasis on the individual human being as the focal point of development, a pragmatic approach of co-operation between the public and private sectors has been followed. The continuity, stability and general framework of moderation, internally and externally provided by the skilful and provident guidance of our affairs by King Hussein since he assumed the responsibilities of his office in the early 1950s, have all permitted the continuation of this approach to economic management. We have tried to mobilize and utilize the best that each of the sectors, public and private, can offer, and have benefited from avoiding the economic consequences of the radicalization and extremism that affected other parts of the Arab East. Our political stance of moderation and centrism has enabled us to adopt an effective economic policy, exploiting our natural and human resources to an extent that would not have been possible within either of the alternative models visible elsewhere, neither through extremism and radicalization, nor within the framework of an authority accepted by economic pressure, with its dependence on the super-development plan and hyper-investment, that has emerged in other parts. Moderation – difficult, at times almost impossible, to sustain – thus demonstrably pays in the long run.

It is pertinent to add at this juncture that behind our approach to economic management lie the Hashemite traditions and principles of leadership. The different components of our society must be allowed to interact positively instead of being subordinated to one social segment rather than others. A qualified arbiter with foresight is more likely to help bring about the best that our society can offer than a manager with vested interests in promoting one element of society above others. It is in this same spirit of the higher Islamic sense of justice, tolerance and equity that the Hashemites, in the different parts of the region, have made their energetic efforts to ensure the security and orderly integration of minorities in the political process of the communities that they govern. Shariffian centrism in politics has its corollaries in economics and economic management. There is a viable alternative to extremism.

On the other hand, we too have had our share of the bad side-effects and excesses, inevitable and perhaps at times self-inflicted, that accompany swift economic growth. But the fact that we can objectively identify and discuss such factors gives us hope that we can successfully undertake the necessary adjustments. Rapid urbanization, regional imbalances, inflation, speculative investments, housing shortages and conspicuous consumption are all amongst the long list of the negative side-effects of rapid economic development that can be discerned in varying degrees in our emerging socio-economic pattern. Rather than attempt the counter-productive course of rectifying such deviation by decree, we have followed a different and more positive approach based on practical measures: among these are more effective regional planning, the creation of centres for new growth in the country, like those in the Jordan Valley and in Wadi Araba, more effective environmental and zoning controls, incentives to farmers, manpower planning, family planning, taxation and monetary policy. These are only some of the methods open to us of adjusting the socio-economic consequences of growth. I believe we have a better chance of achieving the necessary corrective action through such an approach rather than through any drastic or extremist measures.

The future economic potential in the Arab East

Six decades have elapsed since the end of the First World War, when, as we have seen, a political process of immense complexity began to unfold in the modern life of the Arab East. Economically, a great deal has been achieved during this period, and especially in its latter part, when the economies of the different states have exhibited, to varying extents, expansionary trends. In the latter part of these decades, and as the political process gathered momentum and acquired a further complexity through its entanglement in the Arab–Israeli conflict, an even more powerful twist was given to the political and economic course of events by the abrupt advent of the oil boom. This phenomenon has significantly modified the geo-economic parameters that have determined the life of the Arab East since ancient times; it has, furthermore, reacted upon the political process itself, through the side-effects of the economic policies it has stimulated or made possible. Not only had the socio-economic systems of the different states within the region suddenly to deal with the challenge and burden of enormous financial resources; at the same time, the threats facing these states, individually from within and collectively from without, increased in nature and number by geometric progression.

The first generation of Arabs, who experienced the hopes and disappointments of the years between the two World Wars, saw by 1949 the ultimate shattering of their dreams in more senses than one: the failure of democratic experiments, fragmentation from within and failure in the first round of the Arab–Israeli conflict. The next generation of Arabs in the three decades after 1948 passed through an even more rapid and diverse succession of events, beginning with the Nasserist phase of rekindled hopes, soon to be extinguished by the Six-Day War of 1967, and swiftly followed by the new expectations and tensions of the oil boom. This, by the early 1980s, seemed to be flattening out, due to economic indigestion and recession on the one hand, and the rise of fundamentalist extremism on the other. Has this journey of the generations taken the Arab as an individual back to square one?

As the twentieth century runs to its close, what can be done to capitalize on any economic gains that have been achieved so far and to rectify the bad side-effects of increased economic growth? Can anything be done to improve the chances that the last two decades of this century will yield widespread benefits and stability after the turmoil and upheavals suffered by the different nations in the human crucible of our region since the First World War?

The individual as the focal point

I believe a necessary condition for achieving the reorientation that we need involves focusing our attention once more on the "individual" in the Arab East, for whose benefit and for whose "better life" both political and economic action were mobilized in the first place.

If the individual becomes and remains the central point of

economic development plans, not only at state level but also in the direct application of the plan in local regions, there will be some hope of achieving a framework for more effective political and economic action in the coming years, building on complementarities, containing excesses and providing alternatives to extremism.

As we have seen, the consequences of polarization confront the Arab East today not only within its different states, but between state and state. Trade amongst the different states of the region is really insignificant, compared with trade with other parts of the world, especially with the industrialized countries. There is an automatic division of the region into its oil-producing and non-oil-producing members, but every state within these two divisions zealously attempts to reduce the impact both of that division and of the other states in general on its internal political affairs. Yet these apparently divisive factors tending towards polarization in the economic and political fields are in reality transcended by certain unifying characteristics. The aspirations of the people to reconstruct a glorious past and the response or reactions of governments to these aspirations within the different states are remarkably similar.

The increased regional mobility of labour, especially between the oil and non-oil countries, and the transmission of substantial private and official financial resources across the different state boundaries, have created, if not unifying factors, at least causes of common concern and interdependence. Whatever the political orientation of the different regimes in power in the different states, they all share the similar aspirations of their people, and face the common side-effects of the oil boom on their economies and the oil-rush mentality on their populations. In this connection, it is worth noting that such inter-regional transfers even trickle through the occupation boundaries erected by Israel on the West Bank and in Gaza; remittances from Palestinians working in the oil-producing countries still manage to reach relatives back at home.

Regional complementarities and the existing state system

The industrialized nations of the world have become increasingly aware of the fact that each cannot pursue its domestic policies in isolation from the others. I believe that by paying attention to the individual human being in the Arab East an awareness can be created amongst the leaders of our different states of the extent of their economic and political interdependence. Such an awareness is a necessary condition for the development of a framework for organizing, in a coherent manner, the financial and human resources within the region for the benefit of the entire populations of its different states.

The negative side-effects of rapid economic growth have affected the individual, both at state and regional levels. At state level, we have already discussed the usual list of negative factors accompanying swift growth: rapid urbanization, inflation, housing shortages, conspicuous consumption and so on. At regional level, exporting and importing the individual as a commodity and in large numbers has had a negative influence both on the migrating individual and on the people of the importing country.

While the regional mobility of labour has its benefits, there is a need to reinforce these by evolving an investment programme for the individual at regional level. It will be disastrous if the individual is regarded at regional level merely as an input to the investment plans of the recipient countries; explicit regional investment programmes must be developed for the benefit of that individual. While remittances have benefited the Egyptian, Jordanian or Syrian balance of payments, they have not helped reduce the slum areas around Cairo, Amman or Damascus. In certain respects, indeed, such remittances may have augmented these tendencies. The continued existence of the slum areas in the capital cities of the Arab East is only one example of the factors that will not only affect the individual and the decision-maker in the labour-exporting countries, but will ultimately affect both in the labour-importing country.

The problem that has to be addressed is the lack of a complementary economic strategy that binds the oil-producing states with the manpower-rich states of the Arab world. Inequality in income and wealth is a cause of resentment, recrimination, instability and discord in the region. The tension which has characterized the relationship between the governments of these states is gradually filtering down to affect the attitudes of their public. A major factor in determining the nature of this relationship is the fact that the bulk of the Arab population lives in non-oil-producing countries, which are not adequately compensated for the contribution that they make to the oil-producing countries through the educated and technically skilled manpower that they export to them. The outlook of the intelligentsia in these states discourages those with new wealth from investing more widely in this region and tends towards a self-centred approach to its problems. Although the Arab summit conference at Amman in 1980 adopted a joint Arab economic strategy and declared the "development decade", neither has made an important impact at popular level.

Wealth, of course, should not be measured by the possession of a balance in other peoples' banks only. It is also the acquisition of a national capacity to organize and produce goods and services in order to generate a surplus of both. It is for these specific reasons that competent financial management in the Arab East will have to be obtained and developed. The present lack of this expertise has caused the lack of expansion of banking and investment relationships between the oil producers and the others. The Western framework of finance that has been formulated over many centuries and matured in the West has been superimposed on the economies of the Third World, including the Arab states. The historical lesson that should have been drawn from the previous bankruptcy of Khedivial Egypt or the Ottoman state is that strength lies in the capacity to organize, mobilize and manage financial resources and obligations. Unfortunately, this capacity has not been developed at a rate that will keep pace with the acceleration in the development of similar skills in the Western world.

Security through a Middle East development framework

A regional framework for development can be evolved through identifying regional plans for different sectors based on regional complementarities and on providing a better life for the individual at regional level. The water, energy, manpower, transport and communication needs of the different states in the Arab East are interlinked in the long run. While, in the construction of the oil pipeline from the Gulf to the Red Sea, developments at Yanbu on the Red Sea complement developments in the Gulf, the Jordanian south-east provides a potential that can reinforce and link such developments with the north-west. Numerous other areas that offer complementarities, in the form of canals and irrigation, exist in the region between the Nile to the west and the Euphrates–Tigris to the east. Investing in these complementarities need not contradict or conflict with the existing state system in the Arab East. The urban slums around Cairo or Amman or Damascus have an effect, not less real because indirect, on the individual and decision-maker in Kuwait or Riyadh or Abu Dhabi. Investing in the reconstruction of Lebanon, or the West Bank and Gaza, will benefit not only the Lebanese and Palestinian individual, but the individual in the Arab East at large. Security will ultimately depend on achieving progress in these fields rather than on the illusion of military strength.

The West Bank: regional co-operation versus polarization

The theory of international trade tells us about the gains and the higher level of welfare that result from trade. The freer the trade, the higher the gains. Ultimately, through free trade each country would concentrate on its special advantage, thus achieving still higher levels of production and welfare. Besides trade, economic integration and the increased mobility of the means of production that it could achieve would yield further benefits by allowing further specialization and a higher level of efficiency. Needless to say, attempts to apply such patterns in the real world encounter a number of practical but not insurmountable obstacles: we have only to consider the experience of Western Europe, despite the fact that its member states did not start from points of such disparity as exist in the Arab East.

Relative disparities within the Arab East are much more pronounced, to say the least, than in the European Community. Dislocations resulting from prolonged periods of upheaval must be adjusted before a practical start can be made. The situation in the West Bank and Gaza is a case in point. There the prolonged exposure of the domestic economies to the much more advanced (and more highly subsidized) Israeli economy has distorted their economic structure. After 1967, trade barriers were largely removed between the Israeli economy and the West Bank, while a barrier was imposed on trade flows from the East to the West Bank. The sudden imposition of a customs union between two economic entities at widely disparate levels of development imposes an artificial framework on both sides: it has a particularly brutal effect on the infant industries on the West Bank, and reduces or even removes the chances of the emergence of indigenous West Bank industrial enterprises, faced as they are by the more competitive (and heavily subsidized) Israeli industries. The structure of employment both on the West Bank and in the Gaza strip has been dramatically transformed since 1967 due to the fact that an increasing proportion of the labour force finds employment in unskilled jobs within the Israeli economy. There has been no productive investment in the West Bank and Gaza, and because they are exposed to the impact of the Israeli economy while at the same time they are severed, on a partial and selective basis, from the neighbouring Arab economies (and especially from that of Jordan), a lopsided pattern of development has emerged. This pattern must be put right before there can be any real prospect of regional development. Considerations other than calorie intake and the water level come into play in assessing the future of economic co-operation within the region in practical terms.

The doctrine of "basic human needs", so much in vogue nowadays, must transcend economic jargon and be translated into political action if it is to have any real value in the situation confronting us today in the West Bank and Gaza. Self-determination is as much a basic human need, if not more so, than calorie intake. In the absence of such a basic approach, apparently benevolent and humanitarian actions directed at the West Bank and Gaza might yield the opposite result by deepening existing imbalances in the pattern of life that exist today in these territories, and make any eventual accommodation still more difficult to obtain. According to Israeli official statistics, there were about 153,000 persons employed in the West Bank and Gaza in 1970. During that same year, there were about 21,000 persons from these territories employed within Israel. By 1981 employment within the territories had dropped to 140,000, while the numbers of those employed in Israel had increased to 76,000. What is of further interest is the fact that by 1981 more than one-half of that employment within Israel was in construction, in contrast to only 11 per cent in the territories themselves. In 1981 there were about 39,000 persons from the West Bank and Gaza employed on construction sites in Israel, while only about 15,000 persons were employed in construction within the occupied territories themselves. In other words, there were more West Bankers and Gazans building for the Israelis than for themselves. Such thousands of persons commute daily to Israel and return to sleep within the occupied territories. They cannot reside or own property within Israel, while Israelis increasingly "settle" on the West Bank. I do not think this is the type of specialization and welfare that advocates of the theories of free trade and economic integration had in mind. It is perhaps closer to the theory of apartheid.

Marxist theory envisages the division of society into classes on economic grounds and predicts the inevitability of the proletarian struggle. On the West Bank and in Gaza, occupational divisions between the "haves" and "have-nots" further coincide with nationalistic Israeli and Palestinian racial–religious (Jew and Arab) and political (occupier and occupied) lines. Surely this is a pattern of stratification and a recipe for class struggle beyond the wildest Marxian dreams. A development framework for the Arab East that has the individual human being as its focal point, that invests in the individual at regional level, would enable the organized channelling of resources for investment in the West Bank and Gaza for the benefit of West Bankers and Gazans. By re-establishing the severed links between these occupied territories and the region of which they were once part (especially Jordan), an alternative framework can emerge in place of the existing pattern, by which the lives of West Bankers and Gazans are being transformed into a satellite existence as a source of cheap unskilled labour.

Unless the existing framework is changed, any attempt to address the needs of West Bankers and Gazans will in reality push Palestinian and Israeli further along the path of polarization and eventual collision. I am not suggesting that the outcome of such attempts will be to make life so economically unbearable for the West Bankers and Gazans that they will revolt against Israeli occupation. Rather I am pointing out that apparently (or even genuinely) benevolent moves to ameliorate the conditions in these territories under the present circumstances of occupation will in reality yield the opposite result of moving the area closer to the point of instability and ultimate collision. If public figures or decision-makers in the West do not see the point in this argument, it is perhaps because their view is based on shorter-term considerations in which the factors I am addressing do not even arise.

Meagre as its resources are, Jordan has been extending substantial financial support to the occupied territories since 1967. Until recently no questions have been raised about the modalities of this support or its intentions. In the aftermath of the Baghdad summit meeting of Arab heads of state in 1979, a joint Jordanian–PLO committee was set up to organize help to the people of the occupied areas. Arab funds were made available for that purpose. Jordan's co-operation with the committee has had the same aim that prompted the continuation of financial maintenance of public services in the West

Bank since 1967: namely, to enable the people of Palestine to remain in their ancestral homeland. Today, international action is required to join the important conduit of Jordanian assistance to protect the Arab identity of the people of the occupied areas. More than financial generosity is required for this purpose. There is an overriding need for a restatement of the socio-economic requirements of the Palestinian people on their own soil. A comprehensive settlement of the Arab–Israeli conflict will afford such a resolution. The search for peace must continue, especially if, through their industry, the Palestinian refugee community is to make a positive contribution to the development and stability of the region.

4 The Search for Peace

The general situation in the Middle East grows daily more alarming. The terrible events of the last few years have had so grave an impact on the political scene that it will be a long time, if ever, before it will disappear. The threat to the fragile peace of the region is no longer simply local: it is not limited to the immediate area of the clashes between Syrian or Lebanese forces, PLO fighters and the Israeli army, or of the Gulf war between Iraq and Iran. Not far behind is the prospect of an increased polarization, which may lead to a direct confrontation between the two world superpowers, the USA and the USSR.

It is a matter of great concern that the significance of these threats does not appear to have been analysed with any penetration or even appreciated in political circles around the world. The rapid deterioration, the passively accepted fragmentation, which have characterized the Lebanese crisis, have compounded the problem and added a new dimension to the complex enigma of peacemaking in our troubled region. It is not a war by proxies that we fear, but a general outbreak of conflict which may involve the superpowers in the northern and southern tiers of the Middle East. It is too easy to imagine the new horrors that we may all have to face: the new use of deadly weapons, a conflict prolonged by the mutual impact of vast and nearly equal armaments – as in so many instances of "limited confrontation" since the Second World War, it is a battle that no one could win.

The current deterioration is the result of many and divergent regional and international political factors. Chief among these is our repeated failure to tackle the question of

Palestine. For too long the lack of any solution has been allowed to fester and poison the positive development of domestic politics, not only in the Arab states but in Israel as well. The denial of Palestinian legitimate rights has triggered off a fresh wave of extremist political action which could undermine the social tranquillity of other states in the region, just as it has destroyed the social fabric and the centrist politics of Lebanon.

Rarely has the region been so overwhelmed by the threat of Balkanization and by the politics of fragmentation. Some of these affect the internal politics of the different states involved, others the relations between state and state, but all tend to threaten the peace, stability and integrity not just of the Middle East, but of the whole world. While the situation in Lebanon, with its tragic loss of life and the destruction that seems to have no limit, and while the Gulf war which continues to drain the resources of two neighbouring countries, Iraq and Iran, are full of menace, both are overshadowed by the still more vexed problem of the Arab–Israeli conflict.

As the area and violence of these conflicts have grown and their ramifications extended, so serious attempts at peace-making have dwindled and frozen. We no longer hear so much of the "peace process" or the "momentum for peace". Too many nations are now involved and the disengaged are fewer and more pessimistic about the chances that any real or lasting peace can be established. Hence the occasion of this book: in it I hope to take stock of what has taken place, assess its significance and lend any support that may be possible to the cause of peace. The present situation in the Middle East is the outcome of the interaction of so many diverse and divergent political factors, both new and old, that have come to dominate the region in the last decade. A cursory examination of the events of the last few years will point to but a single conclusion: namely, the triumph of extremist politics, whether in Israel or the Arab and Muslim worlds. In Jewish and Muslim societies, politics have become infused by religious extremism and the precepts of religion have been used to produce political fanaticism; the activities of such groups as the Phalange of Lebanon, Gush Emunim of Israel and the Pasdarans of Iran have brought about a violence in the name of religion rarely known in the Middle East.

Populist fanaticism based on religion has had an immediate impact on society and politics in the whole region. The denial of legitimate rights, compounded by the absence of strong central political institutions to safeguard the cultural, ethnic and religious diversity of these societies, has allowed extremism to flourish and dominate the conduct of public affairs. Social diversity has played an ever-increasing part in the struggle between populist movements of different origins and divergent aims.

The politics of fanaticism has released still more violent forces in social conflict and polarization within the community. Primitive perceptions of the ideology of extremist populist groupings threaten to fragment all states in the region, as is occurring now in Lebanon.

The search for peace in the Middle East crisis has been arduous and long. The region has endured war after war, all part of a futile frenzy whose object nonetheless is a peaceful settlement to the still intractable problem of Palestine. Yet our belief in the ultimate possibility of peace has not been shaken. Our commitment has remained total and absolute. Peace with honour and lasting stability has been our objective since the inception of the Arab Renaissance Movement. My ancestors, as well as my country, Jordan, have always been foremost among the Arab advocates of peace and co-operation between the nations of the world.

The past notwithstanding, our adherence to the principle of a just and lasting peace between Arabs and Israel, expressed by UN resolution 242 in 1967 and reiterated in the Fez proposals in 1982 for the settlement of the Palestine question, cannot be in doubt. The position has been made clear repeatedly both by my brother, King Hussein, and myself on a number of occasions. My brother summed up our stance in his statement to the European Parliament at Strasbourg on 15 December 1983, when he said that "Jordan, King, Government and People, have tried their utmost to contribute to the success of several peace initiatives". He went on to declare:

"We have followed every avenue, exploited every opportunity, and bent over backwards to accommodate friend and foe alike to see a just and lasting peace prevail in our troubled region."

Jordan has firmly supported all international initiatives to resolve the Palestinian and Middle East problems. Our cooperation with the United Nations mission of Ambassador Gunnar Jarring, dispatched to the region following UN resolution 242 of 22 November 1967, was total and genuine. It could not be anything else, since Jordan had participated in its formulation and contributed to it. Following the 1973 war, Jordan took an active part in the deliberations of the Geneva Middle East peace conference, chaired jointly by the two superpowers, the USA and the USSR. Jordan also welcomed the joint Soviet–American communiqué of 1 October 1977, just as we applauded the European peace initiative made in the Venice Declaration of 1980. In the same spirit, Jordan appreciated the Soviet call for an international conference to discuss the problems with all the parties concerned, including the Palestine Liberation Organization, designated the sole legitimate representative of the Palestinian people by the Rabat summit conference in 1974.

Jordan disapproved of the Camp David accords of 1978, principally because the formula devised pushed the Palestine question aside and aimed at a partial peace between Israel and Egypt. Although Jordan has not begrudged Egypt the recovery of territory it lost in 1967, the framework for the settlement of the Palestine question provided by the accords has already proved unworkable, since the projected talks on autonomy for the occupied territories have been abandoned. The conclusion of a partial peace has meant the neutralization of Egypt and has, as a consequence, shifted the strategic balance in Israel's favour.

The emergence of Israel as the dominant power in the region, and the threat of war and ruin, as in Lebanon, that this has brought, has plunged Arab politics into complete disarray in which inter-Arab feuds and internecine war has thriven. Still, Jordan, in spite of these setbacks, has maintained its quest for peace and played a constructive role within the Arab community of states to bring about a consensual attitude to peace negotiations. These efforts culminated in the Fez peace plan of 1982. The plan was preceded by the Reagan Middle East peace initiative made in September of the same year.

All these peace provisions have concentrated on two essential elements of the crisis in the Middle East. They attempt to strike a compromise between Israel's paramount requirement for security, while at the same time they call for a just and lasting settlement for the Palestinians. The proposals require Arab recognition for Israel and an acknowledgement by Israel of Arab entitlement to the right of national self-determination for the Palestine Arabs in their own ancestral homeland. These demands appear simple and clear cut, yet they constitute the crux of a problem that has defied repeated attempts to resolve it. The question that has to be addressed concerns the obstacles to peace. If the Arab commitment to a peaceful settlement is not in doubt, it becomes necessary to look into the nature of these obstacles and define their basic characteristics.

It is a strange paradox, but nonetheless true, that the Arabs and the Israelis have exchanged their traditional roles in the Middle East conflict. The road from Khartoum to Fez, the venues of Arab summit conferences in 1967 and 1982 respectively, has marked a continuous movement on the Arab side towards a peaceful conclusion of the Palestinian question. The only obstruction has been the Israeli refusal to exchange recognition for territory, the basis of all peace proposals made so far. At present, it is the Arabs who press for peace and co-existence, while Israel holds fast to the original Arab stance as enunciated at Khartoum. The Arab leaders concluded in the aftermath of the 1967 war that there could be no negotiations, no recognition and no peace with Israel. Today, it is Israel that refuses to negotiate with the Palestine Liberation Organization, refuses to recognize the legitimate rights of the Palestine Arabs in their own homeland and declares a relentless war against any semblance of Palestinian Arab identity.

In this development, the Camp David accords of 1978 marked a turning point for Israel. The ratification of the accords was followed by the conclusion of a peace treaty between Egypt and Israel in 1979. Since then, Israeli leaders have left no one in any doubt about their immediate political objectives and long-term strategic aims in the Middle East. It requires no great penetration or political insight to see that it is no longer the Arab threat to throw the Jews into the sea that causes strife and depresses the peacemakers, but the campaign of the Likud political alliance and its leaders, Begin, Sharon and Shamir, to drive the Arabs back to the desert and return them to their old nomadic way of life. It is this that undermines the stability and security of all states in the region.

It has become too obvious that Israel accepted the Camp David accords in 1978 not because they seemed to provide a framework for a comprehensive settlement of the Palestine question, but as a means to conclude a separate peace treaty with Egypt. It is also clear that to Israel, from the outset, the conclusion of a peace treaty with Egypt had no practical bearing on the Palestine problem. It was simply a settlement of a bilateral dispute between the two states. As such, the peace treaty with Egypt has not been regarded as a first on the way to a general understanding between Israel and its Arab neighbours, especially the Palestinians, but the one and only move to be undertaken. While willing to restore Sinai to Egypt as part of a deal whereby peace could be traded off against territory, Israel has not been prepared to offer similar terms to the other Arab states whose territory its armed forces occupied in 1967. Thus, as soon as the peace treaty with Egypt was ratified, the talks on autonomy for which the Camp David accords made provision were deadlocked and eventually abandoned. Since then Israel has invaded Lebanon, declared war against the Palestinians, annexed the Syrian Golan Heights and asserted sovereignty over the occupied territories of Arab Jerusalem, the West Bank and the Gaza strip.

The advantages which Israel derived from the Camp David accords were enormous. The neutralization of Egypt in the Arab–Israeli conflict not only made an immediate impact on the strategic balance between the Arabs and Israel, but affected the balance of power among the Arab states as well. With Egypt removed, a mood of defeatism and despondency overtook Arab politics. Arab disarray encouraged the romantic irredentist dreams of Menachem Begin, the Israeli Prime Minister at the time, and his associates. The quest for "Eretz Israel" acquired a fresh impetus and became the most prominent feature of Israel's new attitude. Advocates of a compromise solution, like Abba Eban, Moshe Dyan and Ezer Weizman, were pushed aside and intransigent men like Ariel Sharon and Mordechai Ben Porat took over. Begin's electoral victory in 1981 confirmed that Israel was bent on territorial expansionism as demanded by the covenant of the Prime Minister's own party, Herut, which formed the backbone of the coalition that had been in power since 1977. With these men in charge, Israel was no longer interested in peaceful co-existence with its neighbours, remaining within the confines of its own borders, but had set its sights on a grand design for the region, with very far-reaching consequences.

Israel has come a long way since 1967. The country has undergone a fundamental change of view, both of its own position and in its outlook and attitude to its regional environment, under the Begin–Shamir leadership. In 1967, the political leaders of Israel insisted that they did not covet a square foot of Arab territory. All they wanted was Arab recognition of their political sovereignty as a state and peaceful co-existence with their neighbours. This situation has changed radically. Speaking to the Israeli parliament on 2 September 1982, Mr Begin rejected the peace initiative made by President Reagan and triumphantly declared that Israel alone was to determine where its international borders would be drawn. He went on to reiterate that the West Bank would remain under Israeli domination and control for many generations to come. The statement is an expression of an unashamed resolve to incorporate the occupied territories within Israel for the foreseeable future.

Territorial claims made by the Begin–Shamir administration are not the empty rhetorical gesture of a "romantic in the wilderness", as Begin was once described. They are backed by forceful, at times violent, action. An examination of Israel's policy and methods in the administration of the occupied territories indicates the extent of the change that has occurred

111

there in the last few years. The former Deputy Mayor of Jerusalem, Meron Benvenisti, who has analysed the process of this change, has made startling revelations – demographic, economic and about land ownership.

A number of Arab observers and strategists, who take a radical view of popular resistance to Israeli action, believe that time is on the Arab side and that it will be the most decisive factor in Israel's eventual defeat and collapse. Their current frustration with Israel's military success conjures up a vision of further Israeli expansion until the process becomes detrimental to Israel's own security and stability as a state. Seizure of Arab land would increase the demographic pressure and make it progressively harder for Israel to control the situation. The more Arab population Israel has under its domination, the more difficult it will become to administer. As its resources are stretched beyond the limits of administrative capacity, then the Arabs will be in a position to swamp the Israelis and overwhelm them, or harry and harass them, as in southern Lebanon, until they are driven out. This theory has some merits, but is too millennial to inspire much faith. Moreover, the demographic change already taking place in the occupied territories of the West Bank and Gaza points to a different outcome in the immediate future.

For example, Benvenisti shows that the Arab birthrate in the West Bank is 4.4 per cent per annum, but the growth of the Arab population is only 1.4 per cent. The discrepancy between the two figures is due to the constant stream of Arab emigration out of the occupied areas, a trend actively encouraged by the Israeli military authorities there. Upon the Israeli occupation of the West Bank and Gaza in 1967, some 300,000 people, mainly destitute families from the refugee camps, were pushed across the river into Jordan. In the same year, about 100,000 Arabs in Jerusalem were incorporated within the population of the state of Israel upon the formal annexation of the Arab city. Since then, more than 100,000 people have left the occupied territories. In contrast to this, the growth of the Jewish population has been running at the higher rate of 2.2 per cent and steadily rising, mainly due to immigration and the construction of Jewish settlements; 165

of these have been built so far in areas other than the annexed Jerusalem.

It is of considerable significance that the settlers are no longer simply adherents of the extreme religious organization, Gush Emunim, which seeks the restoration of the promised land in accordance with Biblical provisions, but ordinary families seeking cheap housing away from the overcrowded urban centres of Israel. They receive encouragement and assistance from the government of Israel to move into these areas so that creeping occupation will turn annexation into a reality. Financial and other inducements are made to settle the land and bring about what Mr Dayan called "the creation of facts". The government of Israel has shifted its allocation of funds for housing construction to the occupied territories and introduced several incentives for Jews to live there. In 1979 the government built 15,000 units of housing, only 600 of which were in the occupied territories, but in 1982 out of 8000 government-financed units under construction, 2500 are in the occupied areas. The proportion has risen from 4 per cent to an alarming 30 per cent in three years. The declared aim is to have more than 100,000 Jews living in the occupied territories by 1987 in addition to the 110,000 already living in Arab East Jerusalem.

Israeli assertions of sovereignty and settlement activity in the occupied areas do not constitute the only obstacle to a just and lasting peace. Nor is the process of social and political engineering set in motion by the Israeli authorities confined to the field of demography. It has pervaded other aspects of daily life in these areas. The economy of the occupied areas has been a particular target for manipulation. The objective is to render the economy so totally stagnant that it will become completely dependent on Israeli management. There is little doubt that the integration of the West Bank economy has reached undesirable proportions. About 50 per cent of the total labour force in the West Bank is employed in Israel; one-third of this number has worked there for more than eleven years and two-thirds for more than five years. The economy of Gaza has become even more dependent on that of Israel than that of the West Bank. The terrible paradox for the Arabs, and especially those of Palestine, is that the efficient running of the Israeli war machine is sustained by the exploitation of cheap Arab labour: this is what enables Israel to go to war and suppress the attempts of the Palestine Arabs to regain the right to self-determination in their homeland.

The worst of the measures introduced by the Israeli occupation authorities have been those concerned with land ownership. Israel has assumed direct control of 27 per cent of the total land area in the West Bank. This acquisition has not been confined to state registered domains. It has included land owned by refugees expropriated in their absence and requisitioned by the occupation authorities for military purposes. Regional and local authorities have been set up to incorporate the areas of Jewish settlement into Israel by orders of the military government so that they come under the jurisdiction of the Israeli government.

Since 1967 more than 1000 military government orders have been promulgated for the West Bank. Many of Israel's laws have been amended and altered to suit the purposes of the new situation. The overriding aim is simply to blur the legal administrative distinction between occupied and annexed territories. The military government exercises its authority as if it were a permanent sovereign and not an alien occupying power.

The trend is clearly towards a dual legislative, judicial and administrative system, with different treatment for the Jewish settlers and for the indigenous Arab population, both under the ultimate control of the metropolitan government of Israel. The blueprint for a dual society has been drawn up already. It amounts to the unilateral implementation of Israeli laws and regulation. Once the process is completed, Israel would be in a position to claim that it has fulfilled its obligations toward Palestinian autonomy as required by the Camp David accords. Under these circumstances, there would be no need for any further proclamation or legislative action by Israel, since these moves would already have achieved *de facto* incorporation of the West Bank into Israel. It would be made possible by the gradual extension of Israeli jurisdiction over the occupied areas.

However, the expansionist policy of the Israeli government in the occupied territories solves one problem only by creating another, with more serious, tragic and threatening consequences. Israel's approach to the Palestine question points towards a time, not many years ahead, when Israelis will have to choose between compromising the Jewish nature of their state by giving full political rights to an Arab population nearly as big as the Jewish one, or denying them these basic rights and thereby undermining the democratic institutions of the state, or, more drastically, embarking on a campaign to drive the Arab population eastwards across the Jordan river.

There are about 1,300,000 Palestinians living in the West Bank and Gaza. They have become a beleaguered community, threatened with extinction in its own ancestral homeland. More than 100,000 of them have left the country already to seek a living elsewhere, and the Israeli authorities actively encourage an average of 12,000 to do so annually under various pretexts. When agricultural land is expropriated by the occupation authorities, peasants are given twenty-one days to show proof of ownership. The only conclusive evidence accepted in court is a title deed, which few can produce. Under this rule between 55 and 60 per cent of land in the West Bank can be seized. The procedure has become familiar and court-tested. The authorities rarely lose a case. Still more land is requisitioned under the "land-use planning" regulations, which apply to what are regarded as "sensitive" areas, such as the environs of Jerusalem. The object is to limit the construction of housing for Arabs, thus virtually depriving them of their livelihood: by this means the Arab population can be contained and Arabs continually forced to leave the country. Yet, while Arabs are subjected to these restrictions and general harassment, vast zones are set aside and designated as sites for Jewish settlements.

The beleaguered state of the Arab community under occupation since 1967 must be related to the Israeli quest for dominance in the region as a whole. Israeli strategic planners have made their intentions for the future clear. They seek the transformation of the status and role of Israel from a limited

115

part as one of several littoral Eastern Mediterranean states into a regional power capable of "policing" the whole Middle East. The immediate aim is to be self-sufficient in the production of weapon-systems and other sophisticated equipment to guarantee the state's capacity for independent action. In this context, Israel does not necessarily perceive of its role as a client or even an ally of the United States; it wants to maintain its overt military posture regardless of American attitudes or opinions on any particular turn of events. The ultimate objective is to break up the present state structures of the Arab East so that external threats to the Middle East, the old threat from the West or the new threat from the Soviet Union, could be checked by the power and might of Israel, as the major power in the region.

In an address to the Institute of Strategic Studies in Tel Aviv on 14 December 1981, Minister Ariel Sharon outlined Israel's strategy for the 1980s. The approach was both typically flamboyant and extremely aggressive. He dismissed the possibility of living in peace with his Arab neighbours. His view of Arab–Israeli relations is one of perpetual struggle between two nations, Arabs and Jews, for the control of the same territory, Palestine. He also identified Soviet encroachment in the region as a matter of major concern, a direct threat to the security of Israel. Thus, by entwining Arab national objectives and Soviet political ambitions, Sharon reached the easy conclusion that the imagined convergence of Soviet and Arab interest would have a common purpose: the destruction of the state of Israel.

Assuming the mantle of a major power, Israel would have to challenge the Soviet Union and acquire influence in the Middle East and Africa beyond the area of the Arab East. The traditional belt of confrontation between Arabs and Israelis would have to be extended to include what Sharon describes as the hinterland of Israel. This thesis leads to the further conclusion that Israel's national security interests would require an extension of activity, political and, if necessary, military, far beyond the area of direct confrontation that had been the focus of Israeli attention in the past. Israel's new sphere of influence must be enlarged to include such countries as Turkey, Iran and Pakistan, as well as regions like the Gulf area and countries of north and central Africa.

As Israel lacks territorial depth, Sharon proposes the permanent retention of the occupied areas. These are to provide the basis for a defence system with the establishment of populous and high-quality settlements in key border areas in the West Bank, Gaza and the Golan Heights.

Needless to say, such policies make the pursuit of peace a vain quest. But peace is not the object of Israel's right-wing political establishment. It has taken every opportunity (and the rest of the world has grown accustomed to it in recent years) to deploy its military power on every possible occasion in order to subdue the Arabs of the occupied territories and the neighbouring states. The unrelenting premise that "might is right" has become a characteristic feature of Israel's policy. But the use of brute force will never solve the intractable problems that beset Palestine. The acquisition of territory by war is not only a contravention of international law: it also exacerbates these problems and delays their solution still further.

The Palestinians living in the West Bank have been intimidated by Israel and isolated by the indecision of their own leadership. Since Jordan accepted the general Arab agreement in 1974 to designate the PLO the sole legitimate representative of the Palestinians, the people of the West Bank and Gaza have no Arab government on which they can depend to defend their own interests. In general, the governments of the surrounding Arab states have attempted either to keep the Palestinians quiet or to use the Palestinian cause for their own purposes.

The question that requires immediate attention, and which can only be tackled by the international community of nations, is the status of the Arab people under military occupation, particularly while the present Israeli policy of creeping annexation is maintained. The consequences are likely to prove disastrous as long as Israel denies these people the right to national self-determination. This must not be restricted to participation in a free election, as Israel has suggested in certain quarters: it must be based on the whole

117

sum of historical, cultural, social, economic and political rights of a distinct community of people in its ancestral homeland.

There are, moreover, Israelis who would deny these rights not only to the Palestinian Arabs but to all Arabs. In their quest for dominance and power, some of Israel's leaders want to set in motion a disintegrative process in Arab society that would transform it into warring tribes and sects. The many-sided war in Lebanon has been the forerunner of this process. Oded Yinon, a former adviser to Minister Sharon, sees the disintegration of Lebanese society as a model for all the Arab states in the region. In an article published in February 1982, Yinon portrays the Arab world as a collection of ethnic minorities and divided groups, all liable to further division by internal self-destructive crises. Arab society is seen as split up by these dissensions and feuds: it cannot thus constitute a threat to Israel, unless it is backed by the Soviet Union.

Like Sharon, Yinon believes that Israel must deliberately oppose the USSR, and that to do this it must manipulate and intensify the latent conflict which exists in Arab society. Yinon is, of course, at one with some radical Arab nationalists in thinking that the Arab world will not be able to maintain its present framework and must go through genuine revolutionary changes if it is to survive. Both feel that the Arab world is built like a "house of cards", originally put together by Britain and France without taking into account the wishes or desires of the inhabitants. Unlike his Arab counterparts, who seek the establishment of one nation-state extending from the Gulf to the Atlantic on a much firmer and more lasting foundation, Yinon wants to demolish the current structures so that the chaos that has characterized Lebanese politics would pervade the rest of the region. The Arab world, he writes, "was arbitrarily divided into nineteen states, all made of combinations of minorities and ethnic groups which are hostile to one another. Every Arab Muslim state nowadays faces ethnic social destruction from within, and in some, a civil war is already raging."

Where is the logic that leads Israeli strategists to the

118

conclusion that the weakening and break-up of the present states' structure, the destruction of the mosaic into its component parts, would make Israel safe and secure? What myopic strategy makes them suppose that a set of independent fiefdoms and principalities based on ethno-linguistic or religious–sectarian denominations, constantly feuding and warring against each other, could protect Israel from the Soviet threat which they see as the real danger? A brief examination of the history and origins of Soviet involvement in the Middle East points to a very different conclusion. It was exploitation of the regional dynamics of politics that gave the Russians their chance to enter the Middle Eastern theatre. The Arab sense of grievance and injustice over Palestine and the trend towards political radicalism to which it gave rise have been the mainstays of the Soviet influence. The Russians have been able to exploit the Arab–Israeli conflict to insinuate themselves into a position of power and influence. Their penetration of the region will continue as long as Israel maintains its obstructive policy towards the quest for a just and durable peace.

Furthermore, Israel will not be strengthened, as the Israeli strategists suppose, by the fragmentation of the Arab world. That would only give the Russians greater opportunities and a wider field of operations: many new channels for Soviet encroachment would thus be opened. The disintegration of the structure of the present states would add a whole new dimension to Soviet influence, while the prospect of using local feuds to cajole the rival contenders in a war-torn Arab world into their camp would give the Soviet policy-makers the familiar chance to "divide and rule". The USSR would then find it easier to extend its power and attempt to consolidate its influence over the whole region. The state of Israel would be in no position to challenge or check such a Soviet thrust. The only outcome would be increased polarization between the two superpowers, together with their proxies, and, with it, the ever-present danger of direct confrontation.

What is generally overlooked in all this is the fact that Israel itself is not immune from the dangers of political fragmentation. Israeli society, too, is itself a mosaic of more than 100 nationalities, only united by the uneasy bonds of a "garrison state". Ben Gurion thought that the stability of Israeli society and politics could only be maintained by the permanent presence of a "state of controlled tension". Many observers are led to the conclusion that Israel cannot afford to make peace; its evident reluctance conceals a more vital need: a settlement of the Arab–Israeli dispute would certainly deprive Israel of the tension on which its politics seem to thrive. Yet, the body politic of Israel is divided between two major and clear-cut groups. There are the Sephardim, the Jews of the first dispersal, mainly of oriental origin, and the Ashkenazim, who come from Eastern Europe. There are sharp political and ideological differences which both divide and cross these traditional groupings. Recently, social polarization and the latent tensions arising from it have been aggravated by the dire economic situation of the country and the mounting losses in men and material sustained in the war in Lebanon.

The economic direction of a country has always been determined by political decision. Israel is no exception to this rule, but its direction is hardly credible. The fact is that Israel is trying to build an empire on credit. It is practically a bankrupt state, heavily dependent on loans and grants from the USA. Yet American assistance to Israel is employed to the detriment of American interests in the region. The Harvard economist, Professor T. R. Stauffer, has recently shown in a paper published by the Washington Middle East Institute, how much Israel relies on American economic, military and financial aid. Israel currently receives more than 2.5 billion dollars per year in direct official assistance and 700 million dollars more have been requested for 1984 by Israel, making the total official aid 3.2 billion dollars. However, the total transfer of American resources to Israel from both official and tax-deductible non-official sources would raise the figure to about 5 billion dollars. This huge amount does not include the large and increasing short-term Israeli borrowing from American commercial banks, which totals about 2 billion dollars. According to the Central Bureau of Statistics in Tel Aviv, Israel's foreign debt in 1983 stands at 26.5 billion dollars: servicing this debt alone costs 2.5 billion dollars of American aid.

Often, opportunities for peace have been there for the taking, but Israeli leaders have shown extreme reluctance to abandon the siege mentality and the irredentist claims that have characterized their politics. It is as though they do not want to live in the region as partners, but only as overlords. The state of Israel may be *in* the Middle East but its leaders do not wish to be *of* it. Can we wonder at the frustration of President Reagan, who, following the outright rejection of his September 1982 peace initiative, asked: "Can they go on forever living as an armed camp? Their economy is suffering. They have a 130 per cent inflation rate. And they are having to maintain a military presence that is out of all proportion to their size as a nation."

Ever since 1948, Israel has sought the destruction of the corporate personality of Palestine Arabs. Yet the claim to legitimacy of any state of which they are to be subjects is dependent on the extent to which it meets the Palestinians' national demand for a homeland of their own. The eradication of Palestinian national identity will make good the oft-repeated proposition that the Palestine question has no basis in history and no reality in politics. It must be a powerful phantom that has stalked the existence of the Zionist state from the outset, that has caused five major wars between Israel and its Arab neighbours. The Israeli invasion of Lebanon in the summer of 1982, more than any other outbreak of violence, was aimed to lay this ghost, to destroy once and for all the political aspirations of the Palestine Arabs, as embodied by the PLO, the symbol of their national unity.

For the last two years, attention has been increasingly focused on developments in Lebanon as the outlook for a comprehensive settlement of the Palestine question grew dimmer and more remote. However, expectations were raised in May 1983 by the arrival in the region of the American Secretary of State, George Schultz. His approach was direct and innovative, but his efforts have proved, in the event, to be of limited value. The agreement concluded on 17 May between Israel and Lebanon on the withdrawal of foreign troops seemed highly promising at the time. It has not, however, been implemented and this failure has made the situation more dangerous than ever before, especially as it may leave the territorial integrity of Lebanon permanently compromised. Indeed, Israel has decided to redeploy its forces on a more convenient defensive line with the ominous prospect of transforming southern Lebanon into another and larger buffer zone, another West Bank, but in the north.

Israel has not derived much comfort from its military invasion of Lebanon. The so-called "Peace for Galilee" operation may have dispersed and divided the Palestinian combatants and increased the buffer area in the north, but it has done nothing to increase the sense of security of most Israelis, who do not share their government's confidence in the rectitude of their policy. "Quit Lebanon" has become a slogan increasingly popular in Israel, as the occupation army sinks deeper into the Lebanese quagmire, the graveyard of the hopes of every side. Moreover, Israel has lost the free hand it sought in the West Bank, since the invasion has intensified the momentum of Arab resistance to what they see as a blatant attempt at annexation.

The Palestinians' sense of national identity has succumbed neither to Israel's manipulation nor to its threats: their resistance has remained undiminished and vigorous. Rather than accord the Palestinians the right of national self-determination, Israel has supplemented its strategic aim to be the dominant power in the region by seeming to offer an alternative homeland for the Palestinians in Jordan. The obvious object here is to undermine the authority of Jordan and to exploit its vital situation in the Levant to the advantage of Israel. The Red Sea–Gulf region is already in a state of high tension due to the Iraq–Iran war, and the impact of an Israeli strategic initiative in the west could be disastrous.

Thus Jordan becomes the lynch-pin for Israeli strategy, if its exponents are to realize their objective of making their country the dominant state in the Middle East. The cease-fire line round Israel extends to 490 miles, of which 300 abut directly on Jordan. Jordan provides a pivotal link connecting Lebanon and Syria with Saudi Arabia and Egypt. The land

and air routes are of vital interest to Iraq and the northern Gulf states, menaced by the threat of a stridently militant Iran. The acquisition of a position of power in this crucial area would ensure Israeli strategic supremacy over the whole of the Middle East.

It is inconceivable that while Israel resists so vehemently the establishment of a Palestinian state in the West Bank it should contemplate its foundation in Jordan. Such an alternative Palestinian homeland has no substance in history and no basis in law. Until the Mandate over Palestine was awarded to Britain, Jordan was regarded as part of the French concept of *Syrie intégrale* and subject to the jurisdiction of the Arab government in Damascus set up by my great uncle, King Faisal I, in 1918. In 1920, Sir Herbet Samuel, the High Commissioner in Jerusalem, was instructed to keep the area separate from the Mandatory administration. Two years later, Britain entered into agreement with my grandfather, King Abdullah, under which recognition was made of the "existence of an independent constitutional government in Transjordan" under his rule. Jordan became a state before the modern state of Israel was ever heard of.

The substitution of Jordan for Palestine is a device that would serve only one purpose: the destabilization of the country. Look what has become of the suggested alternative homeland for the Palestinians in Lebanon – Jordan would only suffer the same fate. It would undermine the social harmony, economic integration and the political consensus so carefully nurtured since the establishment of the state of Jordan. It would be a recipe for civil strife that would precipitate the spread of extremist politics, satisfy the political aspirations of neither Palestinians nor Jordanians and would render the states of the Arabian hinterland neither safe nor secure. A Palestinian state to replace Jordan would not only contribute to the sense of frustration, sap the political will of people and state, cause the collapse of national institutions as in Lebanon, but it would still leave Israel stalemated.

The intellectual generosity of strategic planners must recognize the role of Jordan and the Arab territories of the

West Bank and Gaza as the middle ground, a thoroughfare for the wealth of the oil-rich south to the populated areas of the north, if and when peace is achieved and the occupation ended. The break-up of Jordan and control by a hostile power would facilitate the exploitation of the central and southern regions as a corridor to the Red Sea and the Gulf states. It must be understood by strategists that respect for the capacity of Jordan's role as complementary to the Gulf states in promoting the Arab identity of Palestine is essential for the maintenance of "constructive management" of Arab public affairs. If political ambitions pursue a course separate from the natural resources of the region, the perimeters of security for the whole Arab peninsula will ultimately be destroyed. The hinterland to the north and the Mediterranean littoral is after all its shield against – or alternatively, the gateway for – penetration and encroachment.

Although Jordan cannot be considered as an alternative homeland for the Palestinians, the close association between the two countries and their peoples should not be completely ignored. The long chain of historical, cultural, economic and political linkages between the two Banks of Jordan cannot be easily broken or abandoned. It has been repeatedly attested by both Palestinians and Jordanians alike. The unity of the two Banks, promulgated in 1950, was based on the exercise of self-determination and the expression of free will. The Jordanian constitution of 1951 stipulated unreservedly that the unification of the two Banks would not prejudice the outcome of a final settlement of the Palestine question. In the meantime, Jordan has remained conscious of the fact that Palestinian national rights would not be forsaken. Those were the principles that guided our action then, and remain to be our guidelines for the future. The Palestinian commitment to continue the closer association with Jordan was reaffirmed by the resolution of the Palestine National Council meeting at Algiers in February 1983 to work towards a confederation between Jordan and the Israeli-occupied territories.

There is little doubt in anyone's mind that Jordan is, and will remain, a natural choice as a partner for the Palestinians, not only in the administration of economic aid in the occupied territories, but also in working towards the determination of their future political status.

It is within this context, as well as to check the rising tide of extremist politics and to contain the politics of fragmentation so prevalent in the Middle East, that Jordan was encouraged by the Reagan peace initiative to embark on a fresh dialogue for peace with the PLO and other Arab partners. It is a fair assumption that the Reagan peace plan, based as it was on UN resolution 242, could have brought an end to the long-festering problem of the Palestine question, had it been pursued with greater vigour and more resolution. Its timing was almost perfect, coming as it did in the wake of the Israeli invasion of Lebanon – a highly tragic and alarming episode in the annals of the Palestine struggle for a homeland. The provisions of the plan were extremely apposite, indicating to both Arabs and Israelis that the USA was totally committed to an even-handed approach towards an eventual settlement of the dispute. Its simplicity was indeed inspired, since it addressed itself directly to the complex issues of the status of the Israeli-occupied territories and of the Jewish settlements constructed since 1967. Unfortunately, the vitality of the plan was allowed to dissipate. With it the momentum for peace was lost.

From the outset, my brother, King Hussein, welcomed the Reagan proposals and wanted to see them evolve and develop. They were not comprehensive enough from our perspective, but marked a refreshing change from previous approaches to a settlement. The injection of a fresh impetus in the peace process was appreciated, as was the President's perception of the Palestinian question as the "root cause" of the conflict in the Middle East. Jordan noted with keen interest President Reagan's interpretation of the Camp David provisions on the status of the West Bank and Gaza strip as essentially part of the Arab patrimony. The omission of a link between Israel's security needs on the one hand, and the recognition of Arab legitimate rights in Palestine on the other, was unfortunate. We had high expectations that the President's call for a freeze on the construction of settlements and concomitant demographic movement in the areas under Israeli occupation would be heeded. It is a matter of more than just regret that despite a total Israeli rejection of the President's initial proposals, action on the part of the American administration to achieve its objectives was not forthcoming.

On its part, what Jordan attempted to do was to combine elements of the Reagan plan, which called for the creation of a Palestinian entity in the West Bank and Gaza, federated with Jordan, with elements of the Arab League plan adopted at the Fez Arab summit conference in 1982, which proposed the establishment of a Palestinian state on the occupied territories under the authority of the Palestine Liberation Organization. Jordan sought an accommodation with the PLO on a joint Palestinian–Jordanian approach for a negotiating stance. The understanding would have been presented to an Arab meeting of heads of state – a summit conference – for endorsement. Under this arrangement, the Reagan plan was to be the vehicle of peace negotiations, while a modified form of the Fez plan would have remained the long-term objective of both Jordan and the PLO. The Fez peace plan would have been redrafted to call for self-determination for Palestinians within the framework of a Jordanian–Palestinian confederation.

A common Jordanian–Palestinian understanding would have made peace negotiations possible but for a number of important considerations, chief among which were, undoubtedly, Israel's rejectionist policy and its adamant refusal to implement legally-binding provisions of international law and United Nations resolutions. From its inception, Israel has charted a deliberate course to undo and undermine every peace plan which might have led to a just and lasting settlement of the Palestinian question. Israeli leaders have waged a constant and relentless war, deploying their enormous military power, to sap the national will of the Palestinian people. The purpose is to alter irrevocably the Arab character of their Palestinian homeland. War, followed by creeping annexation, has become the hallmark of Israeli expansionist policies. Notwithstanding land allocation made under various partition plans since 1937, the current Israeli campaign started with the incorporation of Arab Jerusalem after the 1967 war; it was followed by the annexation of the

Golan Heights. Israel has since staked its claim to the West Bank and Gaza. No doubt, if nothing is done to prevent it, part of southern Lebanon may be requisitioned on security grounds. Not even Egypt, an Arab state which ratified a peace treaty with Israel, has escaped the insatiable appetite for territorial expansion: the still-occupied Taba district of Sinai remains an unresolved issue.

Israel is encouraged in its expansionist tendencies by the apparent American reluctance to give clear-cut support to the fundamental principle of international law which makes the acquisition of territory by force illegal. The USA appears not to regard the Israeli action as a violation of international law. The settlements in the occupied territories have been justified in practice under the pretext that "Jews have the right to settle anywhere". The reluctance of the American administration to act promptly and decisively in its undertaking of peacemaking was a major cause of the failure of the Jordan–PLO talks. The absence of a comprehensive peace strategy has been a feature of American policy-making for almost a decade. In the Arab world it is often interpreted as condonation of Israeli action, whether in the occupied territories or in Lebanon. This view was reinforced at the beginning of this year by the agreement on strategic co-operation concluded between President Reagan and Premier Shamir of Israel. It is expected that increased economic and military aid would make greater funds available for the construction of more settlements in the occupied areas, contrary to the letter and spirit of President Reagan's own peace proposals.

American indecision has allowed Israel to pursue its expansionist policy unhampered. The credibility of the USA as the honest broker in the Middle East has been seriously damaged. American irresolution has made the spectre of superpower polarization loom menacingly large over the region. It has also encouraged Arab radicals and unrepresentative elements within the PLO to challenge the legitimate leadership of that organization. The PLO leadership is not entirely blameless. In an effort to avoid antagonizing the radical wing of its organization, it has been averse to come to an accommodation with Jordan. The avoidance of such a commitment, prompted by a desire to maintain the unity of the PLO, proved futile in the end. The split occurred and factional fighting in the Bekaa valley and northern Lebanon ensued. The fighting was exploited by Syria, whose interest in the recovery of the occupied Golan Heights was ignored by the Reagan initiative.

Syrian pique and Soviet opposition, and their deliberate exclusion from the peace process in the Middle East for a period of several years, combined to obstruct its path. Sole responsibility for peacemaking has been assumed by the United States. Moreover, in the wake of the Israeli invasion of Lebanon, the Soviet Union lost prestige and influence when the Syrian and PLO forces were driven out of Beirut. However, the global role played by the Soviet Union as a superpower is a function of world power politics. As such, the Russians could not be simply relegated to the sidelines of the peacemaking settlement, as the Palestinian people and their representatives have consistently been pushed aside and ignored. A convergence of interests between the Soviet Union and some local powers and forces in the region has made it possible for the Russians to recover their position and challenge the exclusion imposed on their activities. The challenge has become extremely potent in view of the difficulties encountered by the USA in its role as the honest peace broker in the Middle East and the continuous deterioration in the Lebanese crisis.

While American policy-makers focus their attention increasingly on the situation in Lebanon, the outlook for a comprehensive settlement in the Middle East grows more remote. When put in its proper perspective, the Lebanese crisis can be seen as but a symptom of the Palestine question. The conflict in Lebanon falls within three concentric circles. They have a symbiotic relationship: each feeds and fuels the others. At the axis is the Lebanese domestic dimension of the struggle between Muslims and Christians, motivated by the socio-economic disparities between diverse communities and regions and the various ideologies to which they have given rise. The demographic distribution of these elements has given rise to a precarious political system. It can be exploited easily by outside powers and parties of divergent interests and different political orientations. The presence of the PLO combatants in Lebanon has provided the second dimension, and it has introduced the Arab–Israeli conflict with all its ramifications to the Lebanese area. The confrontation between Syria and Israel has given a third and international dimension to the crisis, since the USSR supports Damascus and the USA backs Tel Aviv in its quest for influence and dominance in the region. The overriding fear is thus of a clash between the superpowers themselves rather than between their respective proxies.

The Lebanon has become a major diversion for two potential regional powers, namely Syria and Israel, to pursue their own different objectives. Israel has been able to consolidate its hold on the occupied territories and to continue its intimidation of their people to forsake the land of their forefathers. Syria has engaged in a fratricidal war to contain and control the political will of the Palestinian people. The effect of that war has been to deprive the people of Palestine of the ability, in the absence of functioning public institutions, to articulate the wishes of the principal Palestinian constituency – that of the Palestine Arabs under Israeli occupation. There is no gainsaying that this is detrimental to the peace process, to the Palestinians, to the Lebanese and to all Arabs.

The confrontation between Syria and Israel has brought about a radical shift in the balance of power which is of vital consequence for what I have called the *terra media*, the middle ground of politics between the peoples of the region. Their respective desires to dominate the area may lead Israel to annex formally the occupied West Bank and to leave the territorial integrity of Lebanon permanently compromised. This trial of strength may expose Jordan to mounting pressures from the west as well as the north, accompanied by a further movement of population into the country, due to the social and economic dislocations thus inflicted on the Palestinians both at home and in exile abroad.

The influx of a disgruntled and politically alienated people into Jordan would have an all too predictable effect. It would cause the radicalization of domestic politics and the destabilization of its institutions. The spread of extremist doctrines and projections would destroy the middle-ground position Jordan has so carefully nurtured between the politics of the extremes. The disruption of social harmony in Jordan would only lead towards the radicalization of the whole region as American-backed Israelis and Soviet-supported Syrians battled it out for a position of power and dominance, not only in Lebanon but in the region as a whole. Powerful superpower support would encourage both Israel and Syria to establish strategic links between the Mediterranean littoral and the Red Sea–Gulf theatre, where they would seek to influence the course of future events.

Moreover, the prevailing disarray in the Arab ranks and the absence of a Pan-Arab consensus to address the problems of both Palestine and Lebanon would prevent a conclusive solution: the situation would remain fluid and subject to divergent influences. The charter of the Arab League, which has governed all joint Arab endeavours including all summit activities, has been based on the concept of unanimous agreement on all issues – a constricting approach which the majority of Arabs are determined to rectify as a matter of urgency. However, until this change is introduced, like-minded Arab states may have to act independently of the League's deliberations and decisions.

The people of the occupied areas must be allowed to develop their own institutions to express and defend their own interests. Israel should not – indeed it cannot – be allowed to speak for the Arabs of Palestine. Equally, no Arab state can be a replacement for Palestine or in a position to speak for the Palestinians. Israel must make a choice between peace and territory. The facts of geography and demography impose an interminable dilemma on Israel if it wants to live in peace with its Arab neighbours. It must either compromise the very essence of the Zionist creed or divest itself of the territory it occupies.

There is little doubt that the fighting in Lebanon and the creeping annexation of the occupied territories practised by the Israeli authorities have compounded the continuing impasse over the peaceful settlement of the Arab–Israeli conflict. Jordan is seriously reconsidering the nature of the

Palestine–Jordan familial relationship. Our sole objective, as it has always been, is to protect the Arab identity of the Palestinian people under alien occupation. The preservation of the national character of the Arab community of Palestine will undoubtedly contribute to the maintenance of Jordan's middle-ground position. The revival of our parliamentary institutions will offer all our people a say in the determination of their destiny. We need the help, and require the support, of all to achieve a just and durable peace based on the United Nations' premise of justice for all peoples and security for all states.

Israel should not and cannot be allowed to treat the Palestinian people as though they were an Israeli minority – aliens in their own country. The international community was faced with a parallel problem, history tells us, after the Second World War. The people concerned then were not Arabs, but Jews. When the problem was referred to the United Nations, a special committee on Palestine – UNSCOP – was appointed to ascertain the facts and the validity of the Jewish claims to Palestine and to propose solutions. UNSCOP, in its wisdom, suggested partition. The proposal was not simply an accident of international diplomacy, but one specifically designed to accord the Jews a national identity. It was a recognition of the immutable fact of human geography. It was an admission of the reality of the existence of two nations, not one, in that area – a fact that would have rendered co-existence under a unitary political structure not only difficult, but artificial and pre-carious. Almost forty years later, the Palestine Arabs still await a recognition similar to that awarded to the Jews.

Today the problem of Palestine is as far from a just and lasting resolution as it has ever been. The politics of extremes, the armed struggle advocated by both Arab and Jewish radicals, threaten not only the peace of the Middle East, but that of the whole world. It is a poor world that recognizes only power, not morality, in the conduct of public affairs. The ill-conceived and prudently undeclared policy of the government of Israel is aimed at the eviction of the Arab population of the occupied territories – a policy detrimental to peace in the area, to Western interests, but above all to Israel's own interests.

131

The permanent retention of the West Bank and Gaza, while conferring on Israel certain temporary military advantages, involves obvious risks for its national security in the long run. It also poses serious economic, diplomatic, moral and demographic problems. Further, the Israeli stance on the occupied territories is bound, in the final analysis, to jeopardize and impair the peace treaty with Egypt. Given all these circumstances, Arab–Israeli conflict can only be circular in effect, with no permanent advantage to either side, except to the hardened fundamentalists.

There is a desperate need for urgent action to avert yet another disaster for humanity. In view of the continuing deadlock and the risks that this involves, it is essential that the present situation should not be allowed to drift into worse peril, from which there will be no rescue. There is little doubt that the various parties, both Arabs and Israelis, who are intent on preventing a peaceful settlement, will exploit the opportunity of the present standstill in American peace-making efforts that has arisen from the American presidential campaign. Among the Palestinians and other Arabs, the radicals and extremists will seize the chance to obtain a dominant position and intimidate the moderate peace seekers. The irredentist policy of the Israeli government will gather pace and gain time to achieve its long-standing goal of formal annexation of the West Bank, Jerusalem, Gaza and the Golan Heights.

It is all too clear that the USA, as a superpower, cannot afford to turn a blind eye to these disruptions and dangerous developments. The American interest in the Middle East was not induced by the energy crisis and should not be confined to oil and its availability on the world market, important though it is to the well-being of the West. American concern with the region is a function of the strategic balance between the superpowers and a consequence of world power politics. It would be extremely short-sighted if American interest in the Middle East were to wane and the role of peace broker be abandoned simply because of short-term issues. It is imperative to sustain the interest of the USA in this vital assignment. For this purpose, the creation of a bipartisan peace constituency, as advocated by former Presidents Gerald Ford and Jimmy Carter, becomes an essential feature of American politics. This notion may be augmented by the establishment of a bipartisan commission for the Middle East, similar to the body set up for Central America under the chairmanship of Dr Henry Kissinger – though the commission need not necessarily be headed by Dr Kissinger! The primary purpose of this review commission would be to ascertain the facts and submit proposals which would serve as the basis for American policy and, with it, of an international effort to resolve the Palestine question.

Following the tragic death of the American marines and French troops serving with the multinational peace-keeping force in Lebanon in November 1983, President Reagan has responded vigorously by reaffirming American commitment to a sovereign independent Lebanon, in order to safeguard important American interests in the region. But Lebanon is only one link in a long chain of complex problems. No one should underestimate either the President's obvious resolve or the importance of an independent stable Lebanon, but this goal is not attainable in isolation from the wider issues that have brought the Middle East as a whole to a crisis. The short history of the Lebanese disaster has taught us that tinkering with side issues cannot resolve the fundamental problem. So what is now required of the USA is that it should address the problem itself rather than its symptoms. If this is to be achieved, the Lebanese crisis, including its internal dimensions, must be put in proper perspective. An examination of American interests in stability and peace in the broader context of the Middle East and the Gulf is needed. Military intervention by the multinational peace-keeping forces in Lebanon, and the offshore bombardment by American naval ships, was a dangerous diversion which threatened to pit the military strength of the superpowers one against the other. Their sudden withdrawal has raised serious questions about the credibility of the US role as mediator, since it took place before they could secure an unconditional total withdrawal of all foreign forces from that country. The recovery by Lebanon of complete sovereignty over all its territory within a reasonable time-scale is directly linked to a serious commitment by all factions of the Lebanese people to reconcile their past, present and likely future differences. Only then can there be any hope for a new beginning and lasting peace for Lebanon.

The resolution of the Middle East crisis requires a new and comprehensive peace strategy. International effort should be urgently directed to the underlying source of tension and instability in the region. Its main focus must be the unresolved issue of Palestinian rights in the occupied territories and the Syrian Golan Heights. The obstacles are considerable. Any hope of success will depend upon the determination of the American President to use the full leverage of American power on all concerned. Election year, 1984, seems hardly a propitious time for such an effort, but we hope that the new administration will recognize the dangers and give prompt attention to the need for a comprehensive settlement when formulating its peace strategy for the Middle East.

Jordan is fully prepared to co-operate in this endeavour. We look forward to a serious enquiry into the common problems and challenges that confront us. Our vision of the future is based on complete respect for the provisions of international law and the dignity of man. The guiding principles of our peacemaking efforts are the recognition of the sovereignty, independence and territorial integrity of all states in the region. These principles have been embodied in UN resolution 242, which we still believe provides the broad framework for peace in the Near East. The implementation of resolution 242 could lay solid foundations for peace, mutual confidence and collaboration towards development on the model of Benelux – sovereign states engaged in free co-operation for the benefit of all their peoples. Violent episodes in the history of the region point to a single conclusion: the Middle East cannot survive unless it retains the social diversity it possesses. No one state or group should, or indeed can, establish its hegemony over all the others. Attempts to do so will only prolong the situation we are trying to contend with and avoid.

There is a long chain of historical, cultural, social, economic, political and, above all, familial relationships between the peoples of Jordan and Palestine. Our conception of Jordan, the West Bank and Gaza is that of a *terra media*, a concept of mutual benefit, by which we aim to combine the huge purchasing power of the oil-producing countries of the Arabian peninsula to the south with the skilled manpower and the high technology of the northern region. Our vision is to transform this middle ground into the productive, as well as the experimental, workshop of the Middle East. Given the right conditions, with a just, honourable and lasting peace based on the recognition of basic human rights for all the peoples of the region, as well as security for its states, this vision could become a reality.

It would be no idle boast to suggest, in the spirit of our forefathers, that what we propose could serve as a model for the resolution of the international conflicts among states which abound in the contemporary world. The settlement we envisage will provide for the security of all states in the region, while at the same time safeguarding the Arab identity of the people of Palestine. There is no need to repeat the reasons why any settlement which does not take this essential element into consideration is doomed to failure. It is for this reason that we view with increasing alarm the policy of the Israeli occupation authorities in the West Bank and in Gaza; their approach in Lebanon seems to us to follow an all-too-familiar pattern.

Jordan will continue to play a stabilizing role both internally and in the region as a whole. It will exercise a moderating influence in the context of the Arab–Israeli conflict and remain a conciliatory partner in inter-Arab disputes. Programmes for social and economic reconstruction and development will be maintained under governmental supervision to ensure social justice and harmony. Jordan will remain wary of extremist tendencies and energetic in defusing the conditions that lead to heightened tension. It will persist in its quest for a centrist position, despite repeated condemnation and vilification by extremists on all sides.

Jordan and the other Arab governments want a peaceful settlement to the Palestine question. They seek peace and reconciliation that will allow peoples of different ethnic strains and various religious denominations to live side by side. The meagre natural resources of the region demand the reduction, if not the abandonment, of the huge and expensive defence and armament programmes that hostility has created. These limited resources must be diverted towards economic development and reconstruction.

The time is ripe for a just and lasting settlement of the Arab–Israeli conflict. The prerequisites are clear. The Palestine Arabs, under Israeli occupation and in the diaspora, must be allowed the right to national self-determination. The international community, including the United States, and implicitly even Israel, has recognized that the Palestine problem is at the core of the continuing Middle East tragedy. If it is to be solved, Israel must withdraw from territories occupied in the 1967 war. Withdrawal must be accompanied by the introduction of security measures and guarantees. Normalization of relations, minor territorial adjustments, limitation of weapons and military forces, supervision by multinational observers, demilitarized zones and the other apparatus of peace may become an integral part of a final agreement. Such exchanges, however, must come about as a result of negotiations aimed at mutual security and not through the use of force or the threat of permanent occupation. Whatever happens, the search for peace must go on, not only for the sake of Arab and Jew, but for that of the whole world.

Postscript

Jordan and the American approach to peace in the Middle East

From the mid 1970s, the USA assumed the role of sole mediator, to the exclusion of all others, between Israel and the Arab states. The abandonment of the joint approach with the USSR, which characterized the first phase of peacemaking up to and including the Geneva Middle East Conference, marked an upturn in the American position of power and dominance in the region. However, successive setbacks have eroded that position. Lebanon, the war in the Gulf, the Arab–Israeli dispute: all these have contributed to the frustration of American aims and objectives. The net result has been greater polarization on a global scale and intractable deadlocks in local and regional conflicts.

It is fair to assert that the conspicuous feature of American diplomacy in the Middle East is lack of consistency in the objectives sought, the methods used and the instruments deployed. The approach to peacemaking has been diversified and, therefore, is inherently contradictory. The strategy has been incoherent and confusing, the policies indecisive and the commitment less than resolute. A successful approach must recognize local and domestic political factors, as well as issues of international concern, if it is to defuse crises and resolve the conflict. Concentration on a single aspect can easily be sidetracked by other factors regarded as less important and even irrelevant.

The involvement of the superpowers in such a strategic area of the world is perhaps inevitable, but their approach has often been ambiguous and counter-productive. Dramatic shifts in American diplomacy have taken place either as a function of international power politics or in response to a sudden development in the politics of a volatile region. Occasionally, however, these changes occur because of domestic political pressures in the USA that have little to do with the nation's foreign-policy interest. The deployment of US marines in Lebanon and their sudden withdrawal is indicative of this phenomenon. The approach lacked a clear definition of objectives held in common either with Lebanon or the European powers contributing troops to the multinational peace force: it was marked by contradiction and inconsistency from the outset.

The indecision and irresolution of American policy in the Middle East has been aggravated by the domestic manipulation of the American representative system. The politics of the 1984 Presidential Election Campaign have been exploited by pressure groups such as the American–Israeli Public Affairs Committee (AIPAC) to impose their will on the White House, on Congress and on the candidates seeking election. Calls for the formulation of corresponding pro-Arab organizations to exert pressure on US policy-makers may cause greater contention and make American policy more difficult to discern.

In the last few months before the elections, American officials and elected representatives have been at pains to brush aside what are serious issues of principle for those involved in the conflict as a mere argument about words, in order to secure the electoral backing of Zionist organizations active in US domestic politics. Under their influence, the administration has shifted its ground on crucial aspects of the Arab–Israeli dispute, notably in its changing attitude to the fundamental canon of international law which forbids the acquisition of territory by war. There can be no diminution of this principle, and the double standard applied by the USA casts a long shadow on the American position over Russia's invasion of Afghanistan.

The Congressional initiative to move the US Embassy in Israel to Jerusalem is tantamount to an American sanction of a serious violation of international law. The status of the City is a complex legal issue. Under the British Mandatory administration, sovereignty over Palestine, including Jerusalem, was held in "abeyance" until the establishment of an independent state by the inhabitants of the country. Following the first Arab–Israeli war, in 1948, the country was divided and the legal status of the City became indeterminate, pending a final settlement of the Arab–Israeli dispute.

In 1967, Israeli armed forces occupied Arab East Jerusalem,

which was later annexed. The UN Security Council and the General Assembly have repeatedly condemned the annexation, euphemistically called "unification", as illegal. Israeli sovereignty is questioned in terms of international law. The annexation of the old City *durante bello* must be regarded as null and void. Both the Hague Regulations, appended to the Hague Convention No. IV of 1907, and the 4th Geneva Convention of 1949 contained detailed provisions limiting the legal powers and rights of the occupying power in enemy territory. The distinction between annexation and occupation of enemy territory is given legal status in the Hague Convention No. IV of 1907, in the Law of War on Land and the incorporated Hague Regulations, particularly articles 42–56. As the law stands, the occupying power "does not acquire sovereignty over the territory occupied".

Moreover, the spiritual reverence accorded to the City of Jerusalem by the three monotheistic religions – Judaism, Christianity and Islam – places it above the demands of national politics, ideology or strategy. Exclusive control will deprive it of its spiritual soul. It will not only perpetuate the Arab–Israeli conflict, but will jeopardize American relations with the world of Islam. Compliance with the Zionist-inspired move, which many US administrations opposed in the past, is but an election ploy and one which ought to be resisted. It is nonsense to speak of the anomalous position of the United States Embassy in Israel: for years the American Embassy in Saudi Arabia has been in Jedda, although the capital is Riyadh. No one in Congress thought that was an anomaly which ought to be rectified – a fact that makes the present campaign simply an attempt to prejudge the issue of the status of Jerusalem.

It must be remembered that President Reagan, in his September 1982 initiative, spoke of the immediate adoption of a settlement freeze by Israel to facilitate the peace process. Nonetheless, Israel has been in occupation of Arab lands for seventeen years. Not only has the settlement activity continued unabated, but American funds have been drawn in to finance the work. Both Arab East Jerusalem and the Golan Heights have been annexed in a blatant defiance of international law and of the condemnation of the international community of nations. Israeli leaders of various political opinions have made unmistakable claims to incorporate the West Bank and Gaza into "Eretz Israel". Meron Benvenisti, whose most recent report on the settlements goes so far as to suggest that "the critical point has passed", warns ominously that all the indications point to the development of an apartheid regime similar to that of South Africa.

Despite all this, the attitude of the US administration has been steadily shifting in Israel's favour. The settlement activity was initially considered "illegal", which is what it is. However, it was then regarded as an "obstacle to peace", only to become an "impediment" to solving the Palestine question. If this erosion in the American position continues, the settlements may become, as my brother King Hussein has put it, "just an eyesore". It would be tantamount to the USA abdicating completely from its role as a mediating superpower if, as Mr Richard Murphy, the Assistant Secretary of State, says, the USA refuses to become an agent to pressurize Israel to withdraw.

It is openly recognized that Jordan has legitimate defence and security requirements. However, when it comes to the procurement of the necessary arms from the USA, the American President finds it obligatory to go before an American Zionist audience, organized by the United Jewish Appeal, to justify selling to Jordan. Moreover, in its deliberations on the matter, Congress sees fit to impose humiliating conditions both on the government of Jordan and the US administration in order to enforce measures that are totally unrelated to questions of Jordanian defence and security. Jordan is determined not to make the acquisition of its armaments subject to the whims, desires or approval of Israel and its American supporters. This is not a question of injured dignity but one of principle. Our independent sovereignty and territorial integrity should not be – and we will not allow it to be – secondary to that of Israel.

It is now questionable whether the foundations laid by UN resolution 242 for any peace negotiations are still viable. The Israeli authorities, ignoring nominal American protest, have frustrated every attempt to keep the peace momentum going. While Jordan has been striving for an accommodation with the leadership of the PLO and other Palestinians on the question of a political settlement, Israel has spared no move or measure to prevent this. Nonetheless, and despite threats of Israeli reprisals, a delegation of prominent leaders from the West Bank arrived in Amman in March 1984 to discuss steps towards Jordanian–Palestinian co-operation in this field.

However, the USA failed to press the Israeli authorities to allow 160 members of the Palestine National Council from the occupied West Bank and Gaza to attend a planned session of the Council, whose purpose is to further collaboration with Jordan. Israel is blatantly thwarting the silent majority of the Palestinian people under occupation from exercising its right to self-determination. Yet the American Congress finds it appropriate to reward Israeli belligerence and punish Arab moderation. Is it any wonder that Jordan feels disillusioned with the American approach to peace in the Middle East? It was President Reagan who reiterated the administration's willingness to undertake positive moves, which were clearly called for at a meeting in the White House by King Hussein and President Hosni Mubarak of Egypt in February 1984. But what has been done?

At the same time, Jordan continues to view with extreme concern and alarm the recent measures aimed at extending Israeli law to the occupied territories. These developments constitute a violation of the universally acknowledged provisions of international law and conventions. They also serve as a major stumbling block to peace negotiations. Yet Jordan feels it is imperative that the peace process be kept open and alive, through the United Nations and other intermediaries, in order to retain some flexibility in the situation and to check the growing Israeli tendency to adopt a too rigid, even irreversible, policy towards annexations.

Within this context, Jordan has sought the return of Egypt into the Arab fold, following the Arab boycott imposed after its ratification of the peace treaty with Israel in 1979. The forceful stand Jordan took at the recent Islamic summit, held in Casablanca, in favour of Egypt's readmission to the Organization of the Islamic Conference is an indication of our endeavour to strengthen and reinforce the peace constituency in Arab politics. The meeting between President Mubarak and Mr Yasser Arafat, Chairman of the PLO, following the latter's departure from Tripoli in Lebanon, was appreciated because of the positive contribution Egypt could make to the search for a solution to the Palestine question and to peacemaking in the Middle East.

There is little doubt that co-ordination between Jordan, Egypt and the PLO will require both Arab and international support, however partial or lukewarm that may be. Support must focus on the resolution of the question of Palestine, the root cause of the

Middle East conflict. Egypt's desire to return to the Arab fold is not doubted, but its participation in a joint Arab endeavour on the peace front must be genuine, not limited to gaining Pan-Arab favours and enhancing its potentially influential position in inter-Arab politics, without adding its influence and active support to-wards ending the conflict. The purpose of collaboration with Egypt is to put her experience to the service of all peoples and states in the region in the exploration of fresh avenues and the search for new instruments of peacemaking.

Egypt's moral and diplomatic weight could also be used to resolve the crisis of Lebanon. From whatever viewpoint it is examined, the Lebanese problem must be traced to the much more intractable difficulties stemming from the Arab–Israeli dispute and the ques-tion of Palestine. Israel invaded that unfortunate state, undermined its sovereignty and violated its territorial integrity in order to de-stroy the Palestine national movement, symbolized by the presence of the PLO, and entered on a plan for the Balkanization of the area which threatens all its states, including Israel. The people of Lebanon continue to suffer humiliation, persecution and foreign occupation through no fault of their own.

In addition to resuming the dialogue with the official leadership of the PLO, Jordan is also undertaking informal consultations with several groups of West Bank leaders to sound out their views and sentiments. Of paramount consideration is the fate of the people under Israeli occupation and the eventual status of their land. The Arab community of the occupied territories has felt beleaguered and isolated, constantly intimidated by creeping annexation. Today, the danger of imminent displacement and expulsion stares them in the face, exemplified by the Ben Porat plan for relocating the refugee population of the occupied areas. West Bank leaders are only too well aware of this threat to their Arab identity. They realize that time is running out.

This crucial aspect of the Palestine question has been the focus of the talks between Jordan and the PLO during the last few months. Their purpose is to reach a joint policy for rescuing the land and saving the people. There has been agreement on common objec-tives, but negotiations will continue to determine the practical steps that may lead to total collaboration. The understanding between Jordan and the PLO must be based on a combination of elements from the various instruments of peacemaking available to date. Central to the talks have been UN resolutions 242 and 338, as elaborated by the Arab Fez peace plan and the Reagan September 1982 peace initiative. Every one of these stipulates that all states in the region shall have the right to their own security and territorial integrity, as well as acknowledging the legitimate rights of the Palestinians to a homeland of their own.

Jordan has not only undertaken these discussions with various segments of the Palestinian people and their representatives, but has also been in close touch with other Arab partners to promote a consensus on a peaceful settlement of the talks and, with it, the evolution of common understanding between the Arab states directly involved in the conflict. Since the current state of disarray in Arab ranks is a major obstacle, the formation of a joint approach is the necessary foundation upon which the negotiations can build a comprehensive resolution of the Palestine question and a general solution to the problems of the Middle East. It is realized that the requirement of unanimous Arab decision, as demanded by the charter of the Arab League, is a serious limitation and Jordan has been advocating amendments with the object of containing dissent by a vociferous minority of member states.

The facts are clear. Jordan, with the overwhelming majority of the Arab world, requires a clear and complete commitment to a just and durable peace upon the lines laid down in the UN resolutions 242 and 338. Israel seized Arab land by force of arms. It has altered its identity, incorporated its people into an alien system by denying their legitimate rights to self-determination, employed insidious means to remove the indigenous populations, mounted a relentless war against its neighbours, violated international law and defied the UN organizations which gave it birth. Yet there are those in American political circles who maintain that the onus to make peace falls solely on the Arabs.

The Arabs reject this logic. The Third World, Muslim and non-Muslim, condemns it. Europe and Japan, the main beneficiaries of Middle East oil, disapprove of it. The Soviet Union and the East European States oppose it and China has disavowed it. It is obvious that if the USA is incapable of an even-handed policy, then the gulf between it and this substantial section of world opinion will only grow wider. Friends and allies of the US will have to initiate their own approach and develop independent policies. It may serve the national interest of Israel to isolate itself deliberately, so as to retain the attention and support of world Jewry. It is not in the interest of the USA, as a superpower, to antagonize the rest of the world. An even-handed approach means that every form of pressure available would have to be deployed on both sides. It would also necessitate the participation of other interested parties in the dispute. Both the USSR and Europe, as well as the United Nations and its agencies, can make a positive contribution to a just and lasting settlement of the problems in the Middle East.

Jordan, however, remains committed to the search for a durable peace. The question is no longer how to negotiate, but what to negotiate. In particular, can the USA still command the political will to be an effective mediator in the Arab–Israeli dispute? At issue is the principle enunciated in UN resolution 242, which calls for the restoration of occupied Arab land by Israel in return for Arab recognition of the Jewish state. The USA must demonstrate that its commitment to this principle is valid and unwavering.

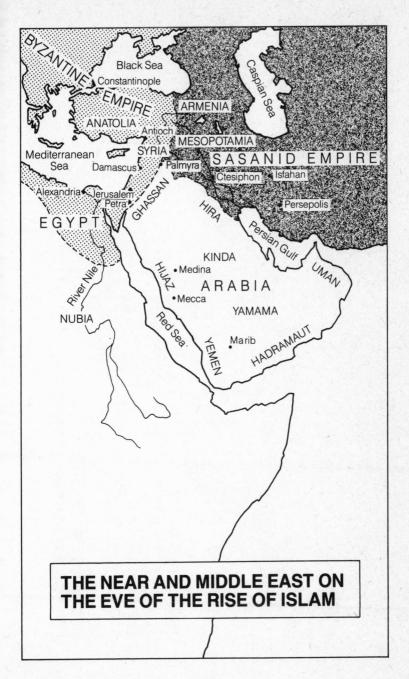

THE NEAR AND MIDDLE EAST ON THE EVE OF THE RISE OF ISLAM

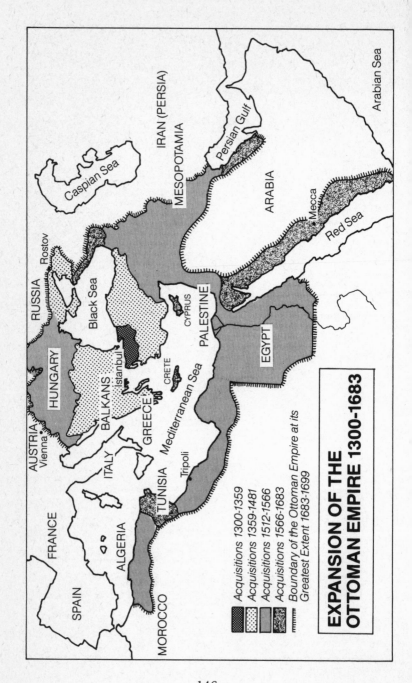

EXPANSION OF THE
OTTOMAN EMPIRE 1300-1683

Acquisitions 1300-1359
Acquisitions 1359-1481
Acquisitions 1512-1566
Acquisitions 1566-1683
Boundary of the Ottoman Empire at its
Greatest Extent 1683-1699

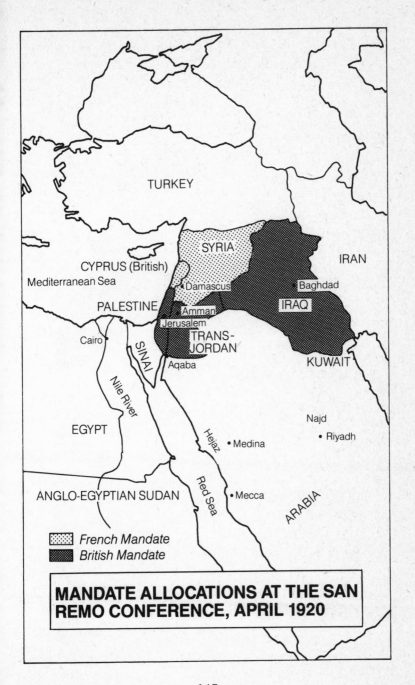

MANDATE ALLOCATIONS AT THE SAN
REMO CONFERENCE, APRIL 1920

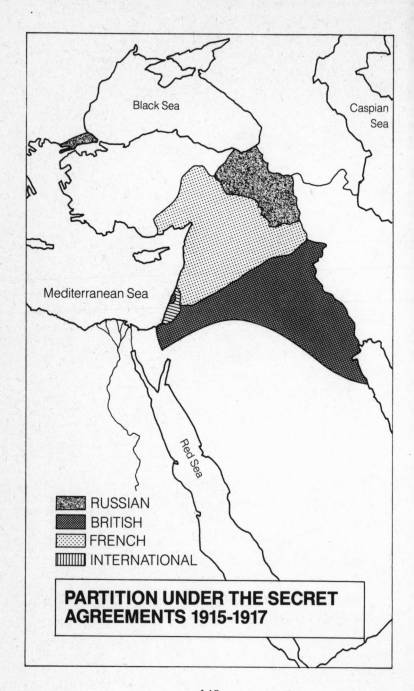

RUSSIAN
BRITISH
FRENCH
INTERNATIONAL

**PARTITION UNDER THE SECRET
AGREEMENTS 1915-1917**

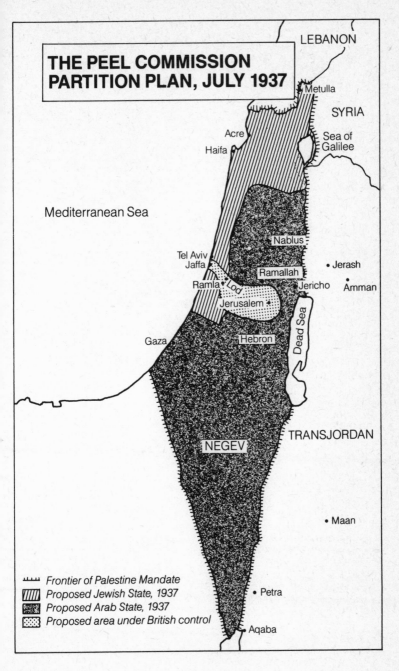

THE PEEL COMMISSION
PARTITION PLAN, JULY 1937

LEBANON

Metulla

SYRIA

Acre

Sea of
Galilee

Haifa

Mediterranean Sea

Nablus

Tel Aviv   • Jerash
Jaffa

Ramallah
Ramla • Lod   Jericho   • Amman

Jerusalem

Dead Sea

Gaza   Hebron

TRANSJORDAN

NEGEV

• Maan

⌐⌐⌐⌐ *Frontier of Palestine Mandate*
///// *Proposed Jewish State, 1937*
▓▓▓ *Proposed Arab State, 1937*
░░░ *Proposed area under British control*

• Petra

Aqaba

149

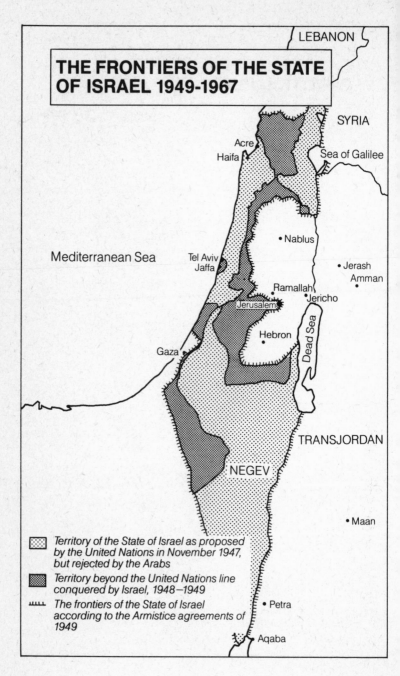

THE FRONTIERS OF THE STATE OF ISRAEL 1949-1967

LEBANON

SYRIA

Sea of Galilee

Acre

Haifa

Mediterranean Sea

• Nablus

Tel Aviv
Jaffa

• Jerash
Amman

Ramallah

Jerusalem

•Jericho

• Hebron

Dead Sea

Gaza

TRANSJORDAN

NEGEV

• Maan

Territory of the State of Israel as proposed by the United Nations in November 1947, but rejected by the Arabs

Territory beyond the United Nations line conquered by Israel, 1948–1949

The frontiers of the State of Israel according to the Armistice agreements of 1949

• Petra

Aqaba

150

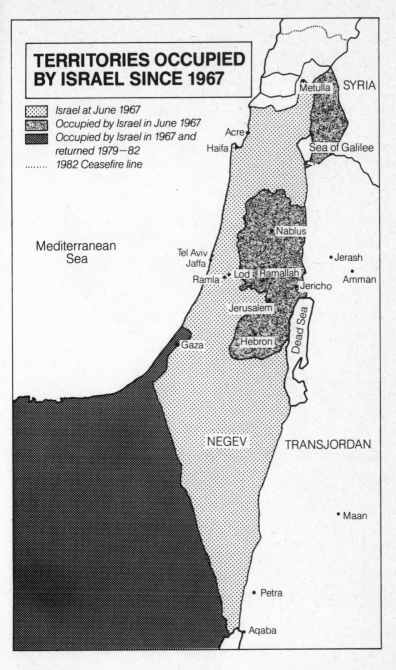

TERRITORIES OCCUPIED BY ISRAEL SINCE 1967

Israel at June 1967
Occupied by Israel in June 1967
Occupied by Israel in 1967 and returned 1979—82
1982 Ceasefire line

SYRIA

Metulla

Acre

Haifa

Sea of Galilee

Mediterranean Sea

Nablus

Tel Aviv
Jaffa

Jerash

Lod   Ramallah

Ramla

Amman

Jericho

Jerusalem

Dead Sea

Gaza

Hebron

NEGEV

TRANSJORDAN

Maan

Petra

Aqaba

151

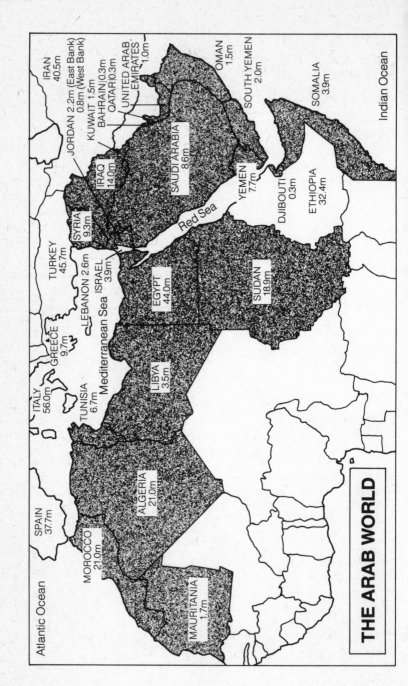

THE ARAB WORLD

Atlantic Ocean

SPAIN 37.7m

MOROCCO 21.0m

MAURITANIA 1.7m

ALGERIA 21.0m

TUNISIA 6.7m

ITALY 56.0m

GREECE 9.7m

Mediterranean Sea

LIBYA 3.5m

EGYPT 44.0m

LEBANON 2.6m

ISRAEL 3.9m

TURKEY 45.7m

SYRIA 9.3m

IRAQ 14.0m

IRAN 40.5m

JORDAN 2.2m (East Bank) 0.8m (West Bank)

KUWAIT 1.5m

BAHRAIN 0.3m

QATAR 0.3m

UNITED ARAB EMIRATES 1.0m

SAUDI ARABIA 8.6m

Red Sea

OMAN 1.5m

SOUTH YEMEN 2.0m

YEMEN 7.7m

DJIBOUTI 0.3m

SUDAN 18.9m

ETHIOPIA 32.4m

SOMALIA 3.9m

Indian Ocean